The paraphrased & comprehendible

The Cloud of Unknowing

newly and loosely translated by Marvin Kananen

2013

A STUDY GUIDE for *The Cloud of Unknowing* is now available for this book.
See sample page at the end of this text.

Ordering information can be found at CreateSpace (book # 4493243),
Amazon, or Kindle

ISBN 13: 978 1493557103
ISBN 10: 1493557106

DEDICATION:
There are certain groups of people and individuals
whose names I will never know:
They are those who truly seek to know more of God,
Those who read and study the Bible,
Those who buy my books,
And, especially,
Those who care about things and people that the world will never
comprehend as having value.
May you be blessed again and again.

Even so, come, Lord Jesus.
The Grace of our Lord Jesus *be* with you all.
Amen.

What is *The Cloud of Unknowing*?

INTRODUCTION

No one knows who wrote *The Cloud of Unknowing*. The book is classified as an anonymously written document. Despite much research, no one has provided more than a speculative answer regarding the identity of the author. Clues to his identity can be found in the text: clearly he was a male theologian and probably a priest, perhaps a monk, perhaps a hermit. Based on several studies of his lexicon, it is quite certain the author lived and wrote from the North-East Midlands of England, presumably the Lincolnshire area or the Lake District.

The late 1300s were both tumultuous and spiritual times. Contemporary theological writers one might be familiar with include Julian of Norwich (1342-1416), Meister Eckhart (1260-1327), Catherine of Siena (1347-1380), Chaucer (1343-1400), Thomas a Kemper (1380-1471), among others. It was during these times the Catholic Church endured two popes (Avignon 1305-1376), England suffered through the Black Plague (1349-1353) and the Hundred Year War (1337-1453), among other events, natural catastrophes, and social changes.

The document itself dates back to the last third of the fourteenth century (Chaucer's century), sometime between 1370 and 1400 A.D. Based on his vocabulary, writing style, and dates, it is also thought this is the first of four manuscripts that are credited to him (the others being *The Book of Privy Counselling*, *Deonise Hid Divinity*, and *A Pistle of Prayer*). Several other documents have been classified as possibly written by the same author.

It seems quite obvious that the author intentionally chose to remain anonymous, although not necessarily from any fear of the church for this work contains no real heresy. It is almost as if the author said, "Let the readers think what they may, but do not ask of my opinion. Seek answers from God, not me."

He intended his book to provide guidance for those rare souls who chose to answer God's calling to lift their lives above the world of sin and to seek God, earnestly and fervently. This book was written directly to an individual (a 24 year-old young man) who seemingly desired to become a hermit. That was then; this book is now directed to another individual: twenty-first century you.

As is stated repeatedly throughout the work, this document was never meant to be publically or freely distributed, but was to be confined to a limited readership. It was intended only for those few individuals God called to rise above the station of being an Active Christian to become a Contemplative Christian.

To summarize the message of the book: there is God and there is the world of Sin. Between them there are two layers of clouds—the lower one being the dark Cloud of Forgetfulness into which the Christian may be drawn, separated from sin. Above lies the dark Cloud of Unknowing that separates our living bodies from God. The author then divides all humanity into four sections, the lower forms are called Common and Special, the upper half are the Singular and the Perfect.

As we rise above the fleshly Common state and become Special (Christians without deep commitment), we are then able to rise to the Singular state which is, itself, divided into two stages of active Christian discipleship—the Actives and the Contemplatives. Then, in one more effort to define these higher levels of Christians on this earth, he divides both levels into two sections, each having a higher and a lower state. The lowest Active is a division of service, the upper Active is Service with Meditation; it is identical with the lower state of being a Contemplative. The highest level we can reach in this lifetime is to be a higher Contemplative. It is for that final group that this book is aimed.

This is not a book aimed at Salvation. It was written for those above the base (Common) state who are already Christians, saved through baptism by the work of Jesus the Christ. This book is given to raise the Christian to a place where there is nothing but God in their heart, mind, soul, and life—an ideal that is no less popular now than when it was written. This work will be meaningful to those who seek a deeper meaning to their lives. It will seem trivial to those who thrive in trivial answers and who seek the easy path.

This translation is essentially a re-write. While the original work and this translation are both written in English, the English of the fourteenth century is barely, if at all, understandable to the twenty-first century reader. For the sake of simplicity, we will call the rewriting of Archaic English to today's English simply a "paraphrased translation."

Ultimately, the book is not theology or philosophy or religious doctrine: it is a book on Christian mysticism. It is meant to be freeing, not frightening. Its message is that it's acceptable to be a Christian Mystic and not be understood by your fellow Christians. Your task is to be true only to God, keeping your eyes on God while letting your example be the teacher that others, likewise called, can follow.

The major resource used in the translating of this book was the work of Phyllis Hodgson. Her 1944 book used the seventeen known manuscripts of *The Cloud of Unknowing*. To this she added an Introduction, Bibliography, Text, Appendices, Notes, and Glossary that made my work possible. Her text, published for THE EARLY ENGLISH TEXT SOCIETY by OXFORD UNIVERSITY PRESS, is still available.

The Transcriber sincerely writes to thank Jeanne Blaszczyk, Jean Wahlstrom, and Bob McGowan for their efforts to produce a book with proper spellings, correct punctuation, complete sentence structure, and coherency that leads to communication. After they finished their work, I was able to restore some of the quaint spellings, punctuations, sentence structures, and other idiosyncrasies that mark this work as undoubtedly my own script, albeit based on the work of another writer, now long-deceased. To these three especially, this writer apologizes for any flaws in this document: *mio sola*, I am the sinner.

Bellevue, WA   Marvin Kananen

12 November 2013

TRANSLATOR'S FOREWORD.

This edition of *The Cloud of Unknowing* is intended to make this great Christian work comprehensible to today's reader. In presenting this paraphrased translation, my desire is to move away from the stiltedly accurate and stodgy editions that have been too difficult to read. Where it was deemed necessary, I have deleted or added words, doing so only for the sake of better communication. Comparable to what I am attempting is to consider the J.B. Phillips paraphrased the New Testament into *The New Testament in Modern English* (MacMillan, 1958)

This book is a "liberal" interpretation. The male pronouns referring to God (but not for the Son, Jesus Christ) have been removed. Also removed were the first person pronouns of the original writer although later in the manuscript my person has been added (called the "transcriber"). The original long chapter titles have been simplified with small word phrases. Also, a single paragraph has been removed from the fifty-fifth chapter and can now be found in the Appendix in the rear of the book).

Here is an example of 14th century English as shown in the fifty-ninth chapter of Phyllis Hodgson's book that reads:

Here biginniþ þe nine & fifti chapi*tre*.

    & ȝif þou sey ouȝt touching þe assenc*io*n of oure Lorde, for þat was done bodely & for a bodely bemenyng as wel as for a goostly, for boþe he assendid v*er*rey God & v*er*rey Man: to þis wil I answere þee, þat he had ben deed, & was clad wiþ vndeedlines, & 5 so schul we be at þe Day of Dome. & þa*n* we schul be maad so 78*b* sotyl in body | & in soule to-geders, þat we schul be þa*n* swiftely where us liste bodely, as we be*n* now in oure þouȝte goostly; wheþ*er* it be up or doune, on o syde or on oþ*er*, bihinde or before. Alle I hope schal þa*n* be iliche good, as clerkes seyne. Bot now 10 þou mayst not come to heue*n* not bodely, bot goostly. & ȝit it schal be so goostly þat it schal not be on bodely man*er*: nowþ*er* upwardes ne donwardes, ne on o side ne on oþ*er*, behynde ne before. ⟨1⟩

Compare this excerpt to the opening paragraph of the current version, showing Chapter 59 below (page 148).

THE FIFTY-NINTH CHAPTER

On this Earth

If you ask anything regarding the ascension of our Lord Jesus as to whether it was done spiritually or physically, it was done in the flesh. Be aware here, what you ask about has a fleshly meaning and a spiritual meaning. He ascended as both true God and true Man, to this I offer a thought for you: He who was dead is now clothed in immortality, as we will be on that Day of Judgment. On that Day, we will be wonderfully re-made in both body and soul. Then we will quickly become whatever we desire to be in the flesh, as we can now become in our spiritual thoughts. This will be true no matter where our thoughts take us, whether up or down, to one side or to the other, behind or before. All these things shall be, we trust, as the scholars say they will be. But for now you will not be able to go to heaven in the flesh, but only in the spirit. It will be as spiritually wonderful as it can be, but not so regarding matters of the flesh which cannot travel upwards or downwards, neither on one side nor on the other, behind or before.[2]

Below is a partial photographic representation of a section from Phyllis Hodgson's *The Cloud of Unknowing*, (p. ii) which shows the original 14th century script, even less readable. This text is from *The Book of Privy Counselling* (MS. Harleian 674 [f. 92[a]])

---

[1] (This is taken from page 110 of Phyllis Hodgson's *The Cloud of Unknowing*, Oxford University Press, 1944).

[2]Marvin Kananen, *The Cloud of Unknowing: Paraphrased & Comprehendible*, Amazon.com, 2013.

INDEX

Section I: The Clouds

Section II: Words

Section III: Martha and Mary

Section IV: The Work

Section VIII: Mentally Arriving

Section IX: Example of the Three

ORIGINAL INTRODUCTION

Ghostly* friend in God, I pray that you have deeply considered the matter of your calling to know and serve God. Truly, I thank God that you, through His grace, confidently stand in the manner of living that you have desired for yourself. May you stand against the coming subtle attacks of your physical and spiritual* enemies. Our ultimate goal is to win that eternal crown of life. Amen.

---

*As words change over time, that which was once called 'goostly' and then updated to 'ghostly' is now called 'spiritual.' Throughout the rest of the book the word 'spiritual' will be used for the word 'ghostly.'

SECTION I: The Clouds

THE FIRST CHAPTER

The Four Stages

Dear friend in God,

This is written to you that you might understand there are four states of Christian living. These four states are: 1) Common, 2) Special, 3) Singular, and 4) Perfect.

The first three of these stages can be done in this life; the fourth, by grace, may begin now but will not be completed in this lifetime. This final state, the Perfection, will continue without end into the bliss of heaven. You can see how these four states have been set here in ascending order, one after the other. This is done in the same manner and by the same steps that our great and merciful Lord has called us, individually and collectively. God is using the very desires that were first planted in our hearts to bring us to earnestly seek holy goal.

From the beginning you knew that you were living just as other Christians, as we all have lived among our worldly and Christian friends. But you have received a special calling that comes from the everlasting love of God. This calling was planted in your heart when God created you before you were born, when you were nothing. Then Jesus bought you with the price of His precious blood when you were lost in the ways of worldly Adam. Our Lord would not allow you to go too far from Him in your manner of living. It was He who kindled a full desire in your heart and He fanned it into a flame of longing. It was our Lord who led you to serve in a unique manner of living, giving you the right to be called His servant. You are the elect.

God has now called you to a place where you can learn to live more spiritually in service than you could ever have imagined previously. God would not leave you in the world, for by the love given you God has always shown a desire for you since before your birth. But why did God do that? Have you never recognized how eagerly and graciously you have been pulled along until you are where you are now, for you would not be reading this book unless you were already through the first two states: the Common and the Special.

This is now the time for you to enter into the third state of Christian living: the Singular. You will soon see that this book covers the manner of living that holds the essence of what you will find in this third state. You have already lived through the first two states. You find yourself in this book now because you are ready to enter into that third state: Singular. Within you now lies a unique call to live in a way where you can learn to lift your foot in love and step forward toward that fourth state, the degree of living that is called the Perfect, the highest state of all.

Welcome, my friend.

THE SECOND CHAPTER

Invitation

Pause now and take a good look at yourself and see who you really are. Do you know? Do you think of yourself as being a wretched weakling? Do you pretend to be someone you are not? Then imagine this: that you would dare to think you are worthy of being called by our Lord to a special task.

It is possible that you are. Are you one of those who has overcome that lethargic and wretched existence that the world would have you bear, living out a life in a sleepy state of unthinking existence? How is it that you have now awakened to seek God and hear this Holy One calling you in love; that you now desire to hear the voice of the divine calling you? Beware, O wretched friend, for the sloth of this world is your enemy.

Were you not content to pretend that you were holier than you really are, as if you deserved God's calling you for this unique life style that you found yourself now investigating? But, in reality, are you not really wretched and afraid? Would you really prefer to do that which is good and right and live fully according to your calling, turning your back to the world?

In truth, you should be meek and loving toward God as you would do with your spiritual spouse. You are talking about the Almighty God, the King of kings and the Lord of lords. Do you think God came down to this lowly station for your sake? And then, do you dare think that from among all the great flock of sheep, God has chosen you to be one of those very special people?

Yes, it is true that you are that precious in God's sight. Apparently, God has set you in the place of pasture where you can be fed with the sweetness of divine love. This is but a foretaste of your heritage, for we are speaking of the kingdom of heaven.

Consider these things, please. Then, when you decide what you should do, do them quickly. From this moment on, you must only look forward and never look back. The easiest way to find personal meekness is to recognize your many failings and do not consider what you possess, no matter how great or how little you might think it is. From now on, and for all your life, you must stand in that desire to please God only if you desire to achieve any degree of that state which God has made it possible for you to be. The desire to be God's servant must come from your own will, a gift placed there by the hand of God Almighty, but done so only with your consent.

Know this, there is one thing we know for certain: God is a jealous lover and will tolerate no other fellowship, unwilling to work in your will unless you belong to God alone. God asks no help, but only to have you completely. The Lord wants you to look only to the one God. You must always guard the windows and the doors of your life from the flies of this world as well as the assault of enemies, for the enemies of God are now your enemies.

If you are willing to do this, then meekly seek God in your prayers and you will soon be helped. Do not be afraid to test yourself and see how well you bear the trials set before you. Or, perhaps, if your fear and dread is too great, you should turn from this book and its lessons that it will offer you. You are free to return to your ways in the world. But know this: God is fully ready and does wait for you.

What should you do now and how will you respond? That is for you alone to answer.

THE THIRD CHAPTER

Cloud of Unknowing

Lift up your heart to God! Keep stirring your heart; keep your mind and heart on God and not on your own goods or on the goods of the world. Do not look upon things that you should not consider, or on anything other than God. Let there be nothing to work evil in your mind but God alone. As for yourself, do not look around but forget the things by which the world would love to hinder you. Keep your thoughts and desires directed toward God. Do not try to overreach any of your thoughts, but let your thoughts be stilled; take no hope in them.

This is an intentional work of the soul to please God. Both the saints and the angels take joy in this work you have chosen, being anxious to help you with all their might.

Likewise, all that is evil will grow enraged when you do what is joyful to God. Evil will try to foul both you and your labors, if it can. Others may be wonderfully helped because of your work, yet neither you nor they will know how much of your effort is really God's work. There is virtue in this work, this work of keeping your heart and mind on God alone. There is no other work for you that can be as virtuous as bringing joy to God. Often the most toilsome work of all can be done quickly when a soul is helped by grace in sensible eagerness. It is known that this is both hard and wonderful for you. Continue in this work.

Do not be slow to begin, but labor in this work until you feel you have lost yourself in that work. The first time you lose yourself there, you will find it to be both a darkness and a blessing. This is your first lesson, the beginning when you first encounter the Cloud of Unknowing.

You will not know what it is, except that you will feel in your soul that this is the place of the pure intent of God. This is a place of darkness but it is not a place of loss. This is a Cloud that will remain above you, between you and your God. Wisely, it prevents you from seeing God clearly by the light of your own understanding or reasoning. You will only feel that divine presence in the sweetness of the love of your affection for God. Before long it will convince you that you want to live in this wonderful darkness as long as you can, ever crying out to God who you love. If you are ever to feel or see God in this lifetime, it is here in the Cloud of Unknowing. It is good for you to be in this Cloud and in this darkness. Although it will probably be a place where you toil as hard you can, it is also a place where you will know God and yourself better.

This is proof of God's mercy for you alone, that you come to this place.

THE FOURTH CHAPTER

Cloud of Darkness

Make no mistake about it, do not attempt to judge this commitment or try to imagine that it is anything other than what it is. It is a serious commitment. If you are willing to continue, hear a little more of what this work involves.

This is real work you have chosen to do. Do not make any mistake about this: it is work. It may not take long before it is completed, for in some ways it is the quickest work that one can imagine. The time it takes may be like the length of an atom, the twinkling of an eye, or the smallest particle of time. It may be so little that it is indivisible and nearly incomprehensible. Yet it is of this brief time that much has been written, but this is the length of time we are talking about: it is the time given to you. After which you will be asked to give an accounting of how you used that time given you.

Is it not a reasonable thing for you to give account of what you have done with your time, whether it is a long or short time given you? In truth, you will be measured in one thing: the strength of your soul or, to say it another way, the power of your own will. This is not merely your willingness or your desires to do what is your own will, but it is your passion to do what is right. On this subject there are probably as many thoughts as there are beats in an hour. Do what is right.

What you are thinking about is almost impossible unless you have been reformed by grace to that first state, the Common state of one's soul as it was before humanity began sinning. You cannot do this on your own, for if you could you would still have this confidence. No, it is only with the help of that same grace that God grants that you can ever hope to be master over your urges and emotions. Only by that grace can one hope to avoid going astray and attain the sovereign state and the controlled will. This is what God desires for you.

With this grace, God gives our soul the full measure of the holy Godhead. In return, our soul gives God the praise of our being and shows our desire to share that passion. God alone and nothing but God is sufficient. More than that is our willingness to fulfill the will and the desires of our soul. For our soul, despite God's reforming grace, is barely able to comprehend the love for which we live. Without that grace, God is totally incomprehensible to any of creation. To wish to know God is the desire of both the angels and our souls, but that would be beyond us except for the love that holds us. Love is, in this case, the only knowable power.

There are two sets of reasonable creatures, angels and people, who uniquely have within them a working power that is called "the desire to know." There is another important working power within them: this second one is called "the power to love." Of these two powers, the first is the power to know God, the one who made you and, ultimately, to realize that God is forever beyond comprehension. The second, the loving power, makes God comprehensible to each of us only so far as a loving soul, by itself and in the virtue of love, can begin to comprehend love in the fullest. This is the love that can fill all the souls and angels who ever existed. This is the endless and marvelous miracle of love. It will never end. God continues to give it freely and will never cease from giving it. It is only by grace that those who may see can see it, for the feeling of this gift is endless bliss, the exact opposite of it is endless pain.

This is why whoever has truly been reformed by God's grace must continue to keep their impulses of the flesh in check. In this life no one will be without some form of these fleshly impulses, yet neither will anyone be without a desire for the taste of the endless sweetness and a desire that is the bliss of heaven. You should not wonder why it is necessary that you toil toward this good work, to know God as best you can. It is this work, as you will understand later, through which we may someday be considered never to have sinned. To this end, we have taken on a task whereby we strive to help God and further the kingdom. It is only through God that we can ever hope to be restored again. Likewise, it is in the failing of this work where one falls deeper into sin and further from God. By continually working on this task alone, without ceasing, one can forever rise, higher and higher, moving farther from sin and, therefore, nearer to God.

Therefore, live as if you keep a good accounting of your time. Nothing is more precious than the time given you. In the little time you have, through God's grace, heaven may be won or lost. Time is a precious token: for God gives time, never twice, but only once. God does this intentionally and will not reverse the order or the course of time given in creation. Time is made for humanity: we were not made for time. God, who is the ruler of nature, will not, in the giving of time, react to the pleadings of our soul; for we live only in the time given us. We will have no excuse for God in our final judgment, nor will we have any reason to not give an accounting of the time we have spent. We will not say, "You gave twice as much time to one person, but I have had only one brief opportunity."

But now you should ask in prayerful sorrow: "What can I do? Is this true what you say, that I will have to give an account of my time spent? I am only twenty-four years of age (ed. note: the actual number may vary depending upon the age of the current reader), I have been too busy to take notice of the time! And even if I could now amend my ways in response to these written words, I could not do it in this world, but need Your grace. Only then may I be able to make amends in the many times that are yet to come. Only then will I know, and yet I know with certainty that of the things yet to come, I shall not do well because of the abundance of my frailty and the slowness of my spirit. I will not be able to keep myself from failing again and again. By this I conclude that I am weak. Help me now, for the love of Jesus!"

It is right for you to say, "For the love of Jesus," for it is only in the love of Jesus that you can find help. Love is such a wondrous power that it makes all things possible. Therefore, if you love Jesus, then all that He has will be yours. He, in his Godhead, is the maker and giver of time. Likewise, He, by his humanity, is the keeper of time. And He, by his Godhead and his humanity together, is the one true judge and the One who will ask you for an accounting of how you spent your time. So bind yourself to Him in love and faith. Then, by virtue of that knot you have tied, you will share with Him and with all that, by virtue of love, has ever been given Him. It is so with us as it was with our Mary who was full of all grace in the keeping of her time, with all the angels of heaven who never lose time, and with all the saints in heaven and in earth who, by the grace of Jesus, account for their time fairly by the virtue of love.

Behold, therein lies our comfort. Understand this cheerfully, that from it you may gain some profit. In these things I give you warning, for no one can truly claim to be a part of the community (that is, the Christian fellowship) with Jesus, his angels, and his saints unless we, with the help of grace, keep an accounting of our time. In this you can be seen as being able to profit, little though it may be, in the fellowship. In this, we must do our own part and we will have our own accounting.

Therefore, take care in this task of keeping yourself time accountable. When you do, you will stand in awe of the marvelous effect this has on your life and soul. For when this is truly conceived and understood, it will come upon you like a sudden prompting which comes without warning, springing up to God as sparks rise from the coals. It is marvelous to count the sweet desires that can rise up in a single hour to a soul disposed to do this work. Combined with the urge to do what is right, one may suddenly and completely forget all that has been created.

But then, as quickly as it happens, as soon as the impulse passes, you will find it was only a corruption of the flesh that brought about the impulse. Once again you will feel the soul fall before some thought, recalling deeds that would have better been left undone or unremembered. But what does this mean? Only this: it wasn't the full answer. Soon afterward, and time and again, other imperfections will rise again as suddenly as they did before. Sadly, these thoughts will rise often.

On this point are many people who think they understand how this works, knowing it is no fantasy or false imagination or quaint opinion. Such people have been brought to reality, not by their devout and blind humility that stirs God's love, but by their own proud, curious, and imaginative wit. This proud, curious wit deserves to be thrown down and crushed beneath the foot, for you are involved in a work that cannot be accomplished mentally but it can only be done in the purity of the spirit.

Whoever hears of this work, either read or spoken, or who imagines that it can come to be by the workings of the mind (for which reason many sit and study how this may be accomplished with a sort of curiosity, thus they war in their imaginations against the natural order, imitating a manner of working which is not profitable, neither bodily nor spiritual). Truly, whoever tries this is dangerously deceived; so much so that even if God, in great goodness, would show this one a merciful miracle and make us leave that evil work, we will soon fall again into other frenzies or other great evils of spiritual sins that are the devil's deceits. Through this error, we can too easily be carried away, both life and soul, and be left without hope. Therefore, for God's love, beware of this evil work and do not struggle in the thoughts of your imagination that only lead you to a worthless end. Truly, grace will not come to them by their own logic. Leave such people and do not work with them.

But do not imagine, although earlier mentioned as a Darkness and a Cloud, that this treasure can be formed as are the mists that float in the air. This is not the kind of Darkness as is found in your house at night when the lights are extinguished. This kind of Darkness and this kind of Cloud can only be imagined with the spirit of your mind. Do not compare them to the brightest day of summer or the darkest night of winter, thinking you will later find a clear, shining light by waiting for a change of seasons. This is only a falsehood of logic. For when I say Darkness, I mean the lack of knowledge as are those things that you do not know or have forgotten. This is the Darkness into which you cannot see without spiritual eyes. This is why it should not be thought of as a cloud of the air, but as a Cloud of Unknowing that lies between you and God, your God.

THE FIFTH CHAPTER

Cloud of Forgetting

If you should ever come to that Cloud, stay there and work in it, as I pray you will. But you must know, this Cloud of Unknowing remains above you and will always stand between you and your God. There is also a second cloud. This second cloud is the Cloud of Forgetting, which is beneath you. It separates you from the rest of creation. This is a good thing.

You may think that you are very far from God because the Cloud of Unknowing stands between you and God; but God is never distant. It is well understood that you were even farther from God then when you had no Cloud of Forgetting between you and the rest of creation. When we speak of "the rest of creation," we do not mean only the physical creatures, but also all the deeds and the acts done by those things within God's creation. We dare not judge any creature, whether in body or in spirit, or consider their condition as to whether they are good or evil, but simply say, as in this case, it is better if they should all remain hidden beneath the Cloud of Forgetting. The Cloud of Forgetting is for our sake, not for theirs and not for God's sake.

Yet though it might be profitable to occasionally think of certain aspects and deeds done in the world, nevertheless, in this work it will generally produce little or no profit. What is the purpose of thinking of the world, and how does that help you to consider those things or the ways of God's creation that are made? These are not spiritual things. Rather, let the eyes of your soul be open and gaze upon God. Even the eyes of a shooter are fixed on the prize as the bowman aims at the target. This is a thing you must know and apply to your life, that of all you think upon, the things of God are far above you. For this current time, there is a Cloud of Unknowing between you and your God. As you are still far from God, there ought to be nothing in your mind but God alone.

Yes, and there is no kind way to say this, it profits you little or nothing to consider the kindness and the worthiness of God or the saints or the angels in heaven, or even the joys in heaven and its promises regarding you. Again, this is to say that we must live with a special beholding to God. Consider that in these other things there is no way to satisfy your purpose. This is the truth, both in this case and in this work. For though it is good to think upon the kindness of God, and to love and praise God, yet it is far better to focus upon God's pure presence, to love and to praise God alone.

SECTION II: Words

THE SIXTH CHAPTER

Stay in the Cloud

But now you should ask, "How can I think of God all the time and think only of God even as I consider who God is?"

To this there is no answer except to say: "I do not know."

With your question, you have been brought to that place which is in both the dark Cloud of Forgetting that is below and that Cloud of Unknowing that is above. This is where you want to reside. For of all the creatures and their deeds—yes, and even of the works of God alone—through grace, this is the only place where one may come to a full understanding. It is here you can consider God, even as you realize no one can understand God. Therefore, leave all the things of the world that you can understand and instead choose to love that One Who you cannot comprehend. For while God may be loved, God will never be understood. God may be found by love and held by our hearts but never by our thoughts. Sometimes it may seem good to think of the special kindness and the worthiness of God. Although from afar it may seem to be a light subject and easy to contemplate, nevertheless, these thoughts need to be cast down and covered by the Cloud of Forgetting. You must learn to faithfully step away from such thoughts and, instead, with the eagerness of a devoted and stirring love, seek to pierce that darkness that is above you. Strike out into this thick Cloud of Unknowing with a sharp dart of longing love. Do not withdraw, no matter what happens.

THE SEVENTH CHAPTER

Finding One Word

If any thought arises that places itself between you and that Darkness that separates you from the things of this earth, it may ask you, "What do you seek? What do you hope to find?" You must simply say, "It is God I desire." Say to it, "It is God and God alone who I desire, for God do I seek, and nothing but God."

If this thought asks you about God, say, "This is the God Who made me and bought me and who has graciously called me to this love." Then say to this thought, "You cannot comprehend God. Go away." Quickly discard these intruding thoughts with the power of your love, even if the ideas your mind presents may seem good and holy, seemingly able to help you find God.

Always be cautious. These thoughts may come to you with fair enthusiasm and wonderful ideas concerning God's kindness. In the beginning, evil will often assure you that God is sweet and loving, full of grace and mercy. Evil does not always lie, but the lies always come later. If you listen to these thoughts, they will assure you they covet nothing; yet, in the end, these thoughts will babble more and more until they bring you far from the way of God's true Passion. These thoughts will promise that you will soon see the wonderful kindness of God; if you listen to them, they will be satisfied. Soon these thoughts, which sounded good, lead you to think about your old, wretched manner of living. Perhaps, in seeing and thinking about these things, the same thoughts will lead you to the same places where you previously wandered. In the end, if you listen to them, you may become so scattered you no longer know where you are or where you were going. The cause of this scattering is that you listened to these thoughts willingly, responded to them, received them, and left God behind even as you sought God. Do not do this.

Yet these thoughts, in their very essence, can seem good and holy. Yes, they seem holy to those who have recently come to contemplate thoughts about God. But they are against any meditations that consider your own wretchedness, the Passion of Christ, or the kindness and the goodness and the worthiness of God. Such thoughts will certainly lead you to err and bring failure to your purpose. It has proven necessary for those who meditate to leave these intruding thoughts behind, to bury them under the Cloud of Forgetting. Choose to consider how to pierce the Cloud of Unknowing that lies above you, between yourself and God. Turn your back on the Cloud of Forgetting.

Therefore, when you begin this work and feel, by grace, that you are called of God, then you should lift up your heart to God with a stirring of that love. Then you will know that it is the God Who made you and bought you and Who graciously has called you to this work. Have no other thoughts about God. Do not even consider these intruding thoughts; it is enough to have a pure intent directed to God. Seek God without any purpose other than finding and serving God.

It might be wise if you can contain this desire in a single word.

This would help you get a better grip on the matter. Find a small word of one syllable; one that harmonizes with the spirit. Find a word like "God," or "Love." Choose either word as you will, or take another as you are inclined, but it should be of one syllable. It is better than a word of two syllables; the shorter it is, the better. Then fasten this word to your heart so that it will never go away, no matter what happens.

This word will become your shield and your spear, whether you ride in peace or to war. With this single word you can beat against the Cloud and the Darkness that surrounds you. With this word, you can beat down all manner of thoughts until they are under the Cloud of Forgetting, hence forgotten. As often as these interfering thoughts press down upon you, even asking you what you have found that is so wonderful, answer it with no word other than this one, simple word. This one word will protect you.

Again, if intruding thoughts offer to give you insight into your chosen word or to expound to you the wisdom of your having selected your chosen word, do not listen. It will tell you the underlying subtleties of that word and praise you for your wisdom of having chosen it. Do not listen. Tell it that you will keep your word whole and unbroken and unchanging.

If you will hold fast to this rule, you may be assured that these thoughts will not bother you for long. And why? This is because you will not let this tempter feed on such sweet meditations as before.

THE EIGHTH CHAPTER

Active and Contemplative Lives

About now you should be asking, "Who is this who urges me in this work?" You should wonder whether this is a good thing or a silly thing you are attempting.

Further, ask yourself, "How could this desire that I work to be nearer to God ever be an evil thing because it can greatly increase my devotion? Are these thoughts not comforting to hear? Sometimes they can make my heart weep for pity at the Passion of Christ, at other times I weep for my own wretchedness. There are many other thoughts I have that seem to be holy and which seem to have done me much good. I think that there is no way these thoughts could be evil. They are good thoughts. This thinking is good for me to consider. I marvel that you should tell me to put them away beneath the Cloud of Forgetting."

These are good questions on your part and necessary to be answered, if possible. First, you ask what this is that encourages you so strongly in your thinking; seemingly it promises to help you in the work. It is probably the native intelligence and perception of your natural mind that imprints itself in your soul by reason of your own abilities. You must consider whether this is good or evil, though usually it seems good in its manner. It may seem wondrous like a beam of light in the likeness of God. But the use of your natural mind may be either good or evil. It is good when it is opened by grace in order to see your wretchedness, the Passion of Christ, or the kindness and wonderful workings of God in all creatures, seeing these things both physically and spiritually. It is easy to believe that this is always good when it increases your devotion as much as you say it does. However, it can also be evil when it causes you to swell with pride and with the curiosity to desire much studying and a passion to learn more of the deceptiveness of letters, as happens with many students. These "insights" can foster a desire to be honored so strongly that they no longer act as meek scholars or masters of divinity or devotion, but they act as proud scholars. This pleases the devil as these same earnest scholars strive to become masters of both vanity and falsehood.

In men and women, whoever they may be, religious or secular, the use and the working of this natural intelligence becomes an evil when it is swollen with pride and the desire to know the worldly things and fleshly conceits. This desire makes them covet the worldly treasures of riches and vain pleasures and the praises of others, but not the things of God.

Then again you may wonder why you would put these wonderfully sounding thoughts beneath the Cloud of Forgetting if they can do so much that is good. Truly, when they are well used they can do you much good and increase your devotion greatly! Here you need to understand that there are only two manners of life in the Holy Church: the first is an Active Life, and the other is a Contemplative Life.

The Active Life is a lower form of the two and the Contemplative Life is the higher form. The Active Life has two degrees, a higher degree and a lower one and the Contemplative Life also has two degrees, a lower one and a higher one. These two life styles have been so coupled together that, though they have always been diverse to some degree, yet neither of them may be fully complete in itself without some part of the other. This is why the higher part of Active Life may actually be the same as the lower degree of Contemplative Life. Therefore, one may never live the fully Active Life without being, at least in part, Contemplative. In the same way the fully Contemplative (as is understood here) is still partly Active. The conditions of the Active Life are both begun and ended in this life: this is not so of the Contemplative Life which begins in this life but lasts without end. In the Bible story of Martha and Mary [see Luke 10:38-42], this is the part that Mary chose and it will never be taken away. The Active Life is troubled and tormented by many details; but the Contemplative Life remains constant in the unity of peace.

The lower part of Active Life serves in a good and honest way, doing the very real works of mercy and charity. The higher part of Active Life and the lower party of Contemplative Life lie in an area of good spiritual meditations with an earnest regard for one's own wretchedness with sorrow and contrition. This state always considers the Passion of Christ and of one's fellow servants with pity and compassion while acknowledging the wonderful gifts, kindness, and works which God has shown to all creation. This is done with many thanks and continual praise. But the higher part of Contemplative Life (as it is called in this life) rests solely in this previously mentioned Cloud of Darkness and in the Cloud of Unknowing, with a rousing love and an obedient faith unto the pure being of God alone.

In the lower stage of the Active Life, one finds oneself to be both outside the self and beneath the self. In the higher part of Active Life and the lower part of Contemplative Life, one finds oneself to be within the self and stable with the self. But in the higher part of Contemplative Life, one is above the self although still under God. In this final stage, one is above oneself in order to win through, by grace, to that place where a person could not come on one's own, that is to be bonded to God in spirit and to become as one with God in love and in accordance to God's will.

Although it is impossible to do this by one's own understanding, one may come to the higher part of Active Life only after witnessing the lower part of that life. Thus it is, when one is first able to come to the higher stage of the Contemplative Life, one is deeply aware of one's former, lower station. This is not necessarily a lovely thing to behold, to sit in meditations upon one's life and see what one's flesh has done, to honestly witness the very things of one's life, both those things that one had done and those things one should not have done. As these workings were never holy works in and of themselves, this becomes an unpleasant thing to witness, even as much as one can understand them. These works were done in the Darkness and beneath the Cloud of Unknowing, often without feeling the affection of the love of God. For now when these thoughts come, it is too late for considering any thoughts or meditations regarding God's wonderful gifts, kindness, or the work in all creation. In both flesh and spirit, these thoughts and meditations will try to squeeze themselves between you and God, although at the time these thoughts might seem to be holy and pleasant and comforting and cleansing. Do not trust them!

It is because of this thinking that I beg you to put down your sharp, subtle thoughts and cover them with a thick Cloud of Forgetting, no matter how holy they may seem to you. They will never help you in reaching your purpose. It is with love alone we may be able to reach God in this life, but never with knowledge, especially our own.

Through all our lives, our soul has been forced to be one with this dying flesh. We have always been tempted by the lure of our own understanding to comprehend the spiritual things, especially those matters regarding God. These vain thoughts will continue to meddle in our spiritual walk in some manner of fantasy until even our works are made unclean. It is no wonder that these, our good and noble-seeming thoughts, actually lead us into greater error.

THE NINTH CHAPTER

Your Mind is a Deceiver

Now, as you increase your understanding, you need to know you will always find yourself continually tempted from within yourself whenever you begin any new work of faith. You must always be on your guard, for you must beat down these urges or they will beat you down. It is true that even when you think you are living securely in this Darkness far above sin with nothing but God in your mind, you need to be aware that your mind is not clean, not even in this Darkness. It is too often filled with thoughts of things other than God. If this is so, and it may not be, but if it is you can be certain that things that seem to be spiritually above you are actually separating you from God. Therefore, put away such thoughts quickly, no matter how holy or good they may seem.

This is most often the truth: ignoring these thoughts will prove to be profitable to your soul. Ignoring them may be a most valuable accomplishment by itself and be pleasing to God and to the saints and to the angels in heaven! The ignoring of these thoughts will even be helpful to you, in body and in spirit, for such is the power of the love of God! This will become a very private love by which you will know the Cloud of Unknowing better. You will be complete for denying these worldly thoughts and you will increase in your spiritual affection for God. It is only when the eyes of your soul are open in contemplation that you can witness the angels and saints in heaven. Only then can you understand the reason for the laughter and songs that are with them in the heavenly bliss.

Do not try to understand the wonder of this, for someday you will see it clearly, but not until you have the strength of grace to reach that state and feel it in this life. Only then you will understand what I am saying. Until then, seek that you may clearly see things that no one of this world has ever seen in this life. Many have had those feelings toward God whose promises have saved us all, but still they fall short, victim of their own vain thoughts. But you, lift up your love into that Cloud. Let God draw your love up into that Cloud where you can prove this and, by God's grace, forget all the things which would distract you.

Keep your pure mind away from anything that is lower than God. Resist the pressures from your will and thinking, they would push you farther from God when you should be coming nearer. In time, if you do not ignore these thoughts, they will make you feel as if you can no longer experience the fruits of God's love. Do you not realize that everything that your mind imagines will draw you away and hinder you in your purpose? Whenever the mind of any special saint or any spiritually pure thing hinders you, you will again find you have the same mind as anyone living out one's wretched life in the world. These things will hinder you and keep you from your real work.

But then, there are some pure and sudden thoughts that are good and clean, spiritual things from God. These are those thoughts that fight against your will and thinking and would draw you, with a sense of warning, to increase your devotions through all manners of ways. Not all thoughts are evil. No, may God keep you from misinterpreting the thoughts that come to you.

As you grow you will understand that although many of the things you encounter seem to be good and holy, yet in some ways they hinder you more than they profit you—if only for a time. What do you seek if you do not seek God perfectly? Do not seek peace of mind like any angel or saint who is in heaven, but seek your peace in God alone.

THE TENTH CHAPTER

Wrath, Envy, Sloth, Pride, Covetousness, Gluttony, Lechery

Seeking peace in God is not what those of the world live for; nor do we do seek fleshly or worldly things as they desire. Those of the world must wonder what is wrong with you when pure and sudden thoughts appear and press against your will and understanding. Then they may come to the strange conclusion that there must be no sin that can be attributed to you. This is something you must deny.

Know this, it is still the pain of the original sin that drives their urges and presses against your being; it is the very sin from which you were cleansed in your baptism. Often these are a sudden passion or thought that needs to be struck down quickly, for your heart is frail and needs to be restrained. Remember that if there is a thing that once pleased you in some manner, it can now grieve you if you dare to consider it. Although these thoughts are usually fastened to the flesh of all living men and women who have been involved in a deadly sin, nevertheless, they will pursue you and all others who attempt to forsake the world and are now pledged to a devoted life in the Church.

Whether these sins are private or public, or if they are of your will or the wisdom of governments, whatever they are, religious or secular, such things in the heart are pardonable sins.

So be careful, for the sins of the world are the source of the fouling of many people's vow to serve God, that vow which was made in the beginning of their service and led to that state where now they stand. This is why vows must always be made before the witness and with the counsel of a discerning elder. Without that discerning mentor, after the vow it may happen that your liking of a particular sin or the resentfulness of your heart in the flesh is carried too long. It may become uncorrected. It will spoil you. Uncorrected, it will fasten to your spiritual heart (that is to say, your will) with your full but unrecognized consent. This is when it becomes a deadly and unforgivable sin.

It may happen that when you read these words, your thoughts might willfully draw your attention to others living in a manner similar to your way of thinking, whether it is a fleshly or a worldly thing. This is especially true of those things that have grieved you before. There may raise up within you a wrathful passion and an appetite of vengeance: this is clearly Wrath. There is another form of foul contempt, the manner of loathing of your person with argumentative and reproachable thoughts; this is called Envy. Or else, if you are in a state of weariness and listlessness of good works, in the flesh or spirit, it may be called Sloth. And if this form of sin is a thing that pleases you, or has pleased you before, there may rise up within you a passionate delight to think about that thing, no matter what it is. Ultimately, if you let yourself rest in that thought, later it will fasten itself to your heart and to your will, and thus you will feed your own heart of flesh to sin.

Did you think that if you coveted nothing of wealth you could live forever in peace and harmony with everything that you contemplate? Is this the thought that you hold for yourself, or do you receive this thinking from what you are told by others? Do you test yourself with the delights of worthiness and kindness and knowing to measure if it is full of grace or of pleasure? If you seek what is full of favor or is something to be fairly heeded, then you need to call this one <u>Pride</u>. If you think about the goods of the world, either about its riches or its cattle, or of those processes which may make one a leader, then it is <u>Covetousness</u>. If it is dainty meats and drinks or any of the delightful things that one may taste, then it is <u>Gluttony</u>. And if it were love or pleasure, or any manner of fleshly dalliance, cajoling, or flattering of any man or woman living in this life, or for yourself, then it is <u>Lechery</u>.

THE ELEVENTH CHAPTER

Deadly Sins

These things are not said because you are known to be guilty or burdened with such sins as you read these words; but because I want you to consider each thought and every reaction you might find stirring within you. All who seek to be closer to God will struggle with some of these things that desire to dampen the stirrings and destroy the thoughts of your heart. Consider these thoughts you are enduring, not in order that you sin, but so that you do not sin. Know this for certain, that whoever does not take hold of the first thought (though they seem to be innocent) will still not avoid the reckless consequences found in forgivable sins. These forgivable sins cannot be utterly avoided in this deadly life. Yet recklessness in those above-mentioned sins, though they are forgivable, should always be avoided by the disciples of our Lord's perfection. Likewise, do not be surprised when others suffer and fall to deadly sins.

THE TWELFTH CHAPTER

Meddling with Intent

As regarding yourself, stand with love and do not fall, never ceasing in your purpose. Remain forever in this Cloud of the Unknowing that lies between you and God.

If you must hate, let your hateful thing be to think of anything that is not God. Do not go where evil things lurk, for this is where sin will work to destroy the ground beneath you and will plant the roots of sin, new and old, in you. It matters not how much you fast, how little you sleep, how early you rise, how hard a surface you sleep on, or how much bitterness you endure. Do not consider such things as if they were lawful, as they are not. It is wrong to put out your eye or to cut out your tongue or to stop up your ears and your nose ever so tightly or to cut off your private members in order to eliminate any manner of temptation. If you try to do painful things to your body, attempting to eliminate any of these vile things hoping that they might help you, they will not. For despite even all that, there would still remain in you the rising and the stirring of sin.

Even if you weep with great sorrow for your sins as well as for the Passion of Christ, or even though you have such great joy for the things of heaven, what can these things do for you? You might think these thoughts surely will do you much good and be of great help, making much profit and showing much grace that will come to you. It is not so. In comparison to the blind stirring of God's love and your desire for God, there is very little which it actually does. Nothing can be done without this stirring of your heart.

This is the part that, by itself, is the best part of Mary's example, without consideration of other things. Those who are without the heart stirring will profit little or not at all. This stirring is not only capable of destroying the ground and the root of sin; it is also able to increase your virtues. However, it must be truly conceived, as all virtues should be truly and perfectly conceived and felt and comprehended in light of this stirring, being without any meddling of vain intent. If one has multiple virtues yet remains without this stirring, their virtues are tainted as if with some crooked intent and are, therefore, imperfect.

Virtue is an ordered and a measured affection that is clearly directed towards God. God is the clean cause and source of all virtues; insomuch that if anyone is stirred to any virtue by any other cause without divine stirring—though it be a major one— yet that virtue, being without God, will forever be imperfect.

This, by example, may be seen in a simple virtue or two; more so than of all the others. Assume that the two major virtues are meekness and charity. These are good, so much so that it would seem that whoever might have these two virtues clearly should need no more: for they would seem to be enough. The one with those two virtues should seem to have it all. They do not.

THE THIRTEENTH CHAPTER

Meekness

Let us pause and take a closer look at the virtues of meekness, both how imperfect it is when it is caused by anything other than God and then how it is perfect when God alone causes it. First, we must know what meekness is in order to see this clearly with understanding and then consider if it can be proved that the truth of Spirit is the cause of this virtue.

Meekness, in itself, is nothing more than the true knowledge and feeling of one's self-worth as one truly is, without deception. For if we can really see and feel ourselves as we truly are, we must be meek.

There are two things that cause this meekness. The first is the filth, wretchedness, and frailty of the human race by which we have fallen into sin. This is the state of sin that we always feel in some manner for as long as we live. It does not matter how holy we try to be, this sin will be with us.

The other cause of meekness is the recognition of the total

overabundance of love and the worthiness of God. The sight and or mere thought of God ought to make us quake and tremble. In comparison to God's worthiness, all clerics are fools and all saints and angels are blind, at least in so much as we see none are, through the wisdom of the Godhead. None are able to be measured by their abilities in manner or in grace against God. Of these things, we dare not speculate how they will be judged.

To consider the opposite, think of God's perfection. It will last without end; all else is imperfection. All we do will only fail us at the end of this life, but this failing may not fall upon the soul within our dying bodies. This is because there is within us a perfection, the result of the abundance of God's grace that has been multiplied by God's desire for us. This happens only as often and as long as God decrees. It is said that, as a result of this grace we receive, we will suddenly have a sense of being lost with a feeling that we have totally forgotten any knowledge that we might have previously possessed. We may be able to feel its absence but not be able to recall what is missing. We will probably be unable to look with understanding as to whether these things have been holy or wretched.

Whether this falls only once, often, or not at all to the soul who is thus disposed, this loss will last for only a short time. In this, the reality is that this may be our first moment of perfect meekness. We will know there is only one cause for this change; the source of this change is God.

If a soul suspects any other cause for this sense of sudden meekness, even though it seems of the highest order, it is still imperfect meekness. Nevertheless, though it sounds like a frightening feeling, it is good and it will always be so. May God forbid you from seeking this grace by any other means.

THE FOURTEENTH CHAPTER

Your Wretchedness

Though we have dared to claim one form of meekness that might be imperfect, the other is based on the true knowledge of the sort of wretched person we truly are. This is the truth that will lead us to the cause and virtue of true meekness most quickly. This is true even if all the saints and angels in heaven and all the people in all the Churches were to pray to God that we might find perfect meekness. This is because it is impossible for sinners to find true meekness or keep any degree of meekness if they think they have gained it by themselves. Without the perfect virtue of meekness, the truth of the self will never be revealed.

Therefore, even by all your toil and sweat for all the things you did, do, or plan to do, it is worthless unless you have a true knowledge and a real sense of yourself as the wretched person you truly are. It is only when you have a true knowledge and sense of God as God is, although you will never know God as God truly is. You will never find yourself to be in bliss, either of body or soul, except as God alone deems it possible. God alone knows what is safe to be known and felt by the meek soul who still must live in this sinful world with our foul bodies.

But do not think that there are only two causes of meekness, one being perfect and the other imperfect. You must learn how to leave the toil of seeking imperfect meekness and find a way of holiness, which alone can direct you toward perfection. As sinners, there is no way to know how to bring this to fruition. However, when you see the greater value of this spiritual exercise over all other exercises, in body or spirit, one can barely understand what can be done by grace. Yet this is how a pure love can be made clean in spirit, even in this Dark Cloud of Unknowing that lies between you and God. Surely this speaks for the perfect virtue of meekness without any special or clear perception of anything under God by which one can know perfect meekness. By this you might take it to be a token of the love in your heart, as it alone can now do for you. For it is by this that you will be meek.

We should often think it is a lack of insightful knowledge that is the cause of much of the pride in this world. Perhaps if one didn't ever try to consider what perfect meekness was, that one could imagine oneself to have already attained perfect meekness. With only a little knowledge and with minimalist thinking, one might imagine this to be true. But it would only be imperfect meekness that one would find. Let us not deceive ourselves or imagine we are fully meek when we are still wrapped up in our own foul, stinking pride.

We must all struggle to attain meekness. It is not a thing that causes those who have it to sin; nor are they likely to ever sin as much or as deeply as they did before.

THE FIFTEENTH CHAPTER

Contrition, Confession, Atonement

Seek that spirit of meekness that it may come to you through God's grace in this lifetime. The seeking of meekness may seem confusing to you, especially if you listen to those who say there is no better way to meekness than by suffering through your own recollections of your wretchedness and previous sins.

It is true that those who suffer through common sins often find themselves, by necessity, humbled by the thoughts of their wretchedness and previous sins. But a time will come when the great rust of their sins is, to a great extent, rubbed away as their conscience grows. Of this we can witness.

There are others who claim they have maintained some degree of innocence. These are those who have never sinned with a will of toleration or by willful intent, but have remained innocent and ignorant until that time they have set themselves apart to be Contemplatives. To both of these groups, their insight and their conscience can bear witness of the change for the better through contrition, confession, and atonement, all three acts that are made only in accordance with the ordinances of the Holy Church. For those who feel called by grace to become Contemplatives (see the Eighth Chapter), there is yet another cause for our humility which must be considered.

We must recognize that, as far above the common life as this new purpose of being a Contemplative is, so was the life of our Lady Saint Mary above the life of the most sinful penitent in the Holy Church. So too, it is as far different from Christ Who is above the life of any other living soul, even as the life of any angel in heaven is far better than the frailty of the life than everyone here who suffers in this world.

But one who truly desires to become a Contemplative can see the way to perfection, and if it is no more difficult than to examine their past, let them seek out and feel their own wretchedness. They seek God, knowing that God has already found them. Then they will discover that this change they seek to make will be a great burden to them. Likewise, those who have never seen their own failings or have never seen themselves as they truly are will never understand the wretchedness of those who have been stirred by sin. They may not know their own shortcomings, yet it is certain that our Lord Jesus Christ, our Lady Saint Mary, the saints, and the angels in heaven all know of their failings. Yet despite this truth, for the sake of this quest for perfection, our Lord Jesus Christ keeps them close to them through the Gospel, the site where those who seek Him find He lives. Again, those who seek Him find Him in the Gospels. Those who would be perfect by grace as He is perfect may find His life in those words.

SECTION III: Martha and Mary

THE SIXTEENTH CHAPTER

Mary's Love

Let no one tell you it is presumptive for you to wish to become a Contemplative. They will gladly and painstakingly point out to you that you have been the most wretched sinner in the world. Too often they will dare to assume—even though you have lawfully amended your way and felt stirred to join that life of a Contemplative, led by your own heart and conscience—that you cannot demonstrate a love toward God. They will assure you that you are not eligible to even enter into that quiet dwelling place in the Cloud of Unknowing that lies between you and your God.

When they confront you, remember what our Lord said to Mary, as if He spoke to all sinners who desire to be called to the Contemplative life, "Your sins have been forgiven you." These words were not spoken to her to cause her sorrow or to remind her of her sinfulness, nor were these words intended to increase her meekness by having her behold her own wretchedness. Then why were they spoken? They were spoken because she loved much! In this we have an example of a pure love that we can only find in the presence of our Lord; it is more precious than all the other works one may seek.

Yet let it be understood that when one encounters great sorrow, there will be found great cause to weep for one's own sins. This is part of the price of merely considering becoming a Contemplative, of daring to live fully humbled by the thoughts of one's own past wretchedness. Even those who have been deservedly wretched while being comfortable sinners all their lifetime may be made hideously and wonderfully aware of the sorrow in their sins. Only then can they be humbled in the recognition of their own wretchedness.

This is true for all of us just it was with Mary.

She felt a deep and heartfelt sorrow for her sins that she would have borne with her all her life, wherever she went. For with her as with all sinners, it was in birth when she and sin were bound together. She may have thought this was a secret matter of her heart, but it was a matter she could never forget.

Nevertheless, it can be said (and affirmed in Scripture) that she felt a heavy sorrow, a sad desire, and a deep grief. She was one who languished in her life for her sins! Her sorrow brought her close to death for the lack of love in her life. Therefore, when she found God's love, she deeply felt the love she found. There is no doubt of this, for it is the condition of a true lover that the more one is loved, the more that one desires to love, even to a state that led her beyond her recollection of her own sins.

She knew fully well about her sin and felt this truth within herself: that she was a most foul wretch, worse than all others. Her sins made a division between her and her God, the very one Who she loved most. This was her motivation; it was the driving force behind her desperate desire to fill that void caused by a lack of love in her life.

Consider this: Did she come down from the heights of desire into the depth of her sinful life, searching through the foul swamp and stinking dunghill of her own sins, examining each sin one by one, recognizing the truth of each, only to weep and anguish over each sin? No, she did not! She didn't because God let her know, by grace for her soul, that she could never bring her own sorrow to an end. For as soon as she could have raised herself to have the ability to repent, she would have sinned again, because she could never have purchased any forgiveness for her own sins.

This is why she had the courage to hang her love and her burning desire in this Cloud of Unknowing. She learned how to love something that she might not see clearly in this life, and most certainly not by the light of understanding from her reason. Yet she felt the sweetness of love in this affection. This was the kind of forgiveness that was so strong that, afterward, she often had little memory whether she had ever been a sinner or not, nor did she care what she had been for the sake of what she had become.

Yes, it is so that she was so deeply affected by the love of Jesus that she took no special attention to the beauty of His precious and blessed body, for He was wonderfully lovely as He spoke and preached before her. She saw Him without regard to sin, either bodily or spiritually, just as He saw her. This is the truth; it says so in the Gospel.

THE SEVENTEENTH CHAPTER

The Active Life

In the Gospel of Saint Luke (10:38-42), it is written that while our Lord was in the house of Martha and Mary, Martha made herself busy with the preparation of the meal while Mary, her sister, sat at His feet. In hearing His words, Mary was not worried about the business of the house as her sister was. Martha's work was both good and holy, as it can be seen to represent the first part of the Active life.

Yet Mary chose to be in the presence of His blessed body and to hear the sweet voice and words of her Master, for this was the better and holier part. In this moment she is seen as being in both the second part of the Active life and the first part of the Contemplative life.

The supreme wisdom of the Godhead remains wrapped in words too difficult for us to understand in our humanness, yet Mary understood with all her heart. For when she saw and heard what was spoken before her, she would not move from there for any reason. Mary sat absolutely still in a sweet and pure feeling of love that lifted her into that high Cloud of Unknowing which was between her and her God.

It is easy to believe there never was as pure a creature in this life, nor ever shall be, as Mary was at that moment when she was so totally ravished by the contemplation and love of God. There will never be a finer illustration of the Cloud of Unknowing as that which then stood between Mary and God.

It was in this Cloud where Mary was occupied with her pure love. It is the best and the holiest place of contemplation that can be found in this life. From this place Mary was not going to be moved for any reason, not even when her beloved sister Martha pleaded with her before our Lord, begging Him to tell her sister to rise and help her. Martha felt she was unfairly forced to do all the work by herself while Mary sat still and did not answer her sister with a word. Mary did not show any resentfulness against her despite the complaints her sister made. Of this behavior there can be no wonder, for Mary had found another work to do, a work that Martha could not understand. For this reason, Mary had no reason to listen to her sister or to answer her complaint.

This story is a key for all these works, these words, and these countenances found in this book that are meant to show our relationship with our Lord. These two sisters are used as an example of all Actives and all Contemplatives who have ever been called to the Holy Church, and so it will be until the Day of Judgment. The work of Mary is understood by all who are Contemplatives, that they should conform their lives to hers. Those who are Actives respond to Martha in the same way and by the same reasoning that she displayed, for the same reasons she voiced.

THE EIGHTEENTH CHAPTER

Those Who Fall Away

As was true when Martha complained about her sister, so today do the Actives complain about the Contemplatives. If there is anyone in this world—religious or secular, it does not matter—who feels stirred to forsake all the things of the outward, worldly business and live fully in the manner of the Contemplative life with a pure conscience, let them. But they need to be aware of this counsel: as soon as their own brothers and sisters, their friends, and all others who do not understand their calling to this manner of life that awaits one who is called, will rise up with a great complaining spirit and stir up many tales, both true and false. There are many examples of those who have fallen from the path because of complaints against them, for those who complain try to make everyone lead the same life as they led before. Sadly, these tales often lead us astray.

It must also be confessed that many people have fallen away from this path even after they chose to forsake the world. They who would have become God's Contemplatives and God's servants, because they refused to obey God in true spiritual counsel, have become the devil's servants and the devil's contemplatives. They have, in turn, led others to become similar hypocrites and heretics, falling into the frenzies and the mischief of the world, to the scandal of the Holy Church.

Of these we choose to cease speaking. They will trouble us no more. Later, if God deems it wise, others will see and recognize these conditions and amend the causes for their great failing. Until then, think no more about them, but let us continue with our matter.

THE NINETEENTH CHAPTER

Forgiveness

There is nothing wrong with Martha; in fact she is a special saint. Her words of complaint about her sister are comparable to those words of people of the world. There is no disrespect meant in comparing her words with theirs. Truly, no disrespect is directed at either sister. God forbid that we should ever say anything that might be taken as a reproach of any servant of God, especially regarding Martha, a special saint, or any of the Actives. She should be fully excused for her complaint, considering the time, reason, and manner in which she spoke. While she did speak those words, it was her lack of knowledge that was the real cause of her misconception. It is no surprise she did not recognize how Mary was occupied; it is possible that as a woman she had never heard anything of this perfection. Also, in what she said and how she said it, she was both courteous and brief. Therefore, she should be forgiven.

This seems to be true of the accusations brought regarding most of the men and women who are living an Active life in the world today. They should also be excused for their complaining words, the sort of grievance we touch upon here. Though all they say might be riotous and boisterous, when they speak they do so without understanding the situation. This is what Martha wished in regard to Mary, her sister, when she complained of her behavior to our Lord. It is in the same manner as people today who know little or nothing of what it means to be a disciple of Christ regarding any who have withdrawn from the business of this world. The world does not comprehend why any would seek to become one of God's special servants in holiness and rightfulness of spirit. If the world could understand them, they would neither act nor speak against those who seek to serve God as they, convinced of their righteousness, now dared to speak. They should also be forgiven, for they know no better manner of living than how they have always lived and worked in the world.

There is need for all who toil to pause and consider their own innumerable faults that everyone has committed in both word and deed because of their own lack of knowledge. We are blessed in that God can forgive us all for our ignorant faults. It serves us best if we believe that other people's ignorant words and deeds can likewise be forgiven. Otherwise, we do not do to others as we would have others do to us.

THE TWENTIETH CHAPTER

Martha Rebuked

Those who set out to become Contemplatives must forgive the Actives for their complaining words. However, it would be better if they themselves should be so occupied in things of the spirit that they took little heed, or none at all, of what other people did or said about them. We should be like Mary, our other example, for even when Martha complained to our Lord about her, Martha behaved as if her sister was not listening to her. If we truly behaved thus, our Lord will do for us as He did when He spoke. He defended Mary.

Our loving Lord Jesus Christ, to whom no secret can be hidden, was required to act as judge by Martha, for she expected Him to tell Mary to rise and help serve in the house. But when Jesus perceived that Mary was fervently occupied in spirit through her love of His Person, He spoke for her. Politely, as was right for Him to do, He answered for Mary, saying that she did not need to go, excusing her because she behaved as she did out of her love for Him. He answered not only as a judge, as Martha requested, that He apply her brand of "righteous" and a "lawful" judgment, but also He spoke as a lawful advocate defending Mary who He loved.

Jesus turned all his attention to Martha, saying, "Martha, Martha." Twice He spoke her name, for He wanted her to stop and truly listen to Him, to heed His words. "You are very busy," He said, "and troubled about many things." For those who are Actives always seem to be busy and troubled by the multiple details of the many things which they feel is their duty to perform, and only afterward are they concerned about the deeds of mercy for their fellow Christians, as charity requires. But this is what He said to Martha, for He would have her understand that her work was good and profitable to the growth of her soul, but she should not think that it was the best kind of work of all the things that a person might do. Therefore He added, "But only one thing is really necessary."

What Jesus was telling her was that God must be loved and praised for God's self, alone and above all other tasks, bodily and spiritually. Further, He told Martha that she should not think that she would be able to love and praise God above all other works because the necessities of this life were keeping one like her too busy. Therefore our Lord spoke words to deliver her from the idea that she might be profitably serving God with both her physical works and spiritual life. She might serve God imperfectly, but never as perfectly as she may have envisioned herself doing. It was for this reason that Jesus said that Mary had chosen the good part, the part that could never be taken from her. For those people who are called to strive for that perfect love, even as it was beginning to be stirred in Mary, they have been stirred by a love that will last forever in the bliss of heaven. For all love is but one love.

THE TWENTY-FIRST CHAPTER
Good, Better, Best

Our Lord said, "Mary has chosen the best[1]." Wherever the "best" is spoken of, it is the third stage after "good" and "better." So it is that "best" is the third number in the order; there is no fourth stage.

Of these three good things, Mary chose the best. There are not three manners of life, for the Holy Church pays attention to only two—the better which is the Active life and the best which is the Contemplative life. These two lives have been privately understood in this story from the Gospel of Luke about these two sisters, Martha and Mary—with Martha as the Active and Mary as the Contemplative. It has been said there are only these two lifestyles if one serves God; but if there are no more than two manners of living, how can one be deemed the "best?"

It seems there are only two lifestyles; nevertheless, in these two lifestyles there are three parts, for there is one between the other two. Of these three, one has already been mentioned earlier in this writing where it was said the first part stands in the good and honest physical works of mercy and of charity. This is the beginning work of the Active life, as it was said. The second part of these two lives lies in the area of good spiritual meditations as one considers one's own wretchedness, the Passion of Christ, and the joys of heaven. The first part here is good, but this second part is the better. This second stage can be seen as either the second part of the Active life or the first stage of the Contemplative life. Here alone the Contemplative life and Active life are actually coupled together like spiritual kindred, as were the maiden sisters seen in the example of Martha and Mary. Thus an Active may come to Contemplation, but no higher; and that happens rarely and only by a special grace. This is also as low as a Contemplative can come towards an Active lifestyle. Here but no lower, and only when the need is great.

The third part of these two manners of lifestyle hangs in the dark Cloud of Unknowing with the others who possess the most pure love for God. God alone puts them there. The first part is good, the second part is better, but this third part is altogether the best. This best part is seen in Mary. As previously mentioned, it is plain to see that our Lord did not say, "Mary has chosen the best part," for there are no more lifestyles than the two. In a choice of two, no one is able to choose the best of three when there are only two options. But of these two lines "Mary has chosen,' Jesus said, 'the best part, that which shall never be taken from her.'

The first part and the second part are both good and holy, yet they end in this life. But it is in the third part, for then there shall be no need to use the works of mercy and no reason to weep for our wretchedness or for the Passion of Christ. For then, unlike now, none will hunger or thirst anymore, or die from the cold, or be sick or homeless, or in prison, or even need to be buried for none will die. It was this third part that Mary chose, or was chosen by grace if you so choose to think.

Whosoever God chooses, let that one listen to these words. For the third part shall never be taken away; and though it begins here in this world, it will continue forever.

Therefore the voice of our Lord cries out to these who are Actives as He calls them now to Himself. He did this for Mary's sake when Jesus spoke to her sister, "Martha, Martha!" It is as if He said, "Actives, Actives! Do as well as you can in the first manner of living and also in the second manner, both in the one and in the other. If you live well and feel so disposed, live in both parts. But do not meddle with those who have chosen to be Contemplatives. You do not know what such a one sees. Allow the Contemplatives to sit down and rest in their thoughts. This is the third and the best part. This is what Mary chose."

---

[1]Please forgive this intrusive footnote. In the Greek Bible the word "good" comes from *agathos*. In the 45 English versions of the Bible examined, 5 translate the word to mean "best;" 11 choose "better;" 17 have "good;" 5 use "right;" and 7 preferred other words or phrases. The anonymous author chose "best" and so we will go with that lest we go afoul with the meaning of Chapter 21. [Data gathered from BibleGateway.com]

THE TWENTY-SECOND CHAPTER
For Love of Mary

The love between our Lord Jesus and Mary was very sweet. She had much love for Him, and He, as He has for everyone who seeks Him, had even more for her. If anyone could have witnessed all the exchanges which passed between them, the reader of the story would find that Mary was so committed in her love for Him that nothing but He could comfort her, nor could anything keep her heart from Him. This is she, that same Mary, who, when she later sought Him at the sepulcher with weeping, would not be comforted by the angels. Even when they spoke to her so sweetly, saying, "Weep not, Mary; for our Lord whom you seek is risen, and you shall meet Him, and see that He is fully alive, and as a friend among His disciples in Galilee, as He is.'" She would not leave or be comforted by their words, for her thoughts were on the King of angels. She was seeking Him and not the words of the angels.

But there is more to the story! Surely whoever will look at the story in this Gospel will find many wonderful points of perfect love written about her as an example for all to follow, perhaps even in this writing. These thoughts have been thought out and written down previously. Surely they are true, fit for whoever can handle them.

If anyone listens in order to hear what is in the Gospel story, they will find the wonderful and special love that our Lord had for Mary, a person who, in her person, was only an ordinary sinner, but one who truly turned from her past. She accepted the grace of Contemplation. The reader will learn that our Lord would not allow any man or woman, not even her own sister, to speak a word against her, as shown when He answered for her. Yes, and there is more! Later He accused Simon the Leper in his own house, for he had dared to have an evil thought against her. This was a great love; this was a passionate love. This is insight into God's love for all who belong and believe and claim to be children of God.

THE TWENTY-THIRD CHAPTER
Enough is All

Truly, we ought to lovingly conform our love and our life to the Lord Jesus, in as much as it is within us. We should strive to be in His grace and counsel, to be like the model of love and loving as shown with Mary. There is no doubt that our Lord will defend us in the same spiritual manner when we need defending. He, as needed, will answer those who seek or think things against us, even those who think these thoughts privately in their hearts.

We ourselves ought not to speak against whatever some say or think against us. We live in the travail of this life; it is why they railed against Mary. We need not regard or give thought to their words or thinking, neither will we give any regard to their words or their thoughts concerning the spiritual nature of our pure work, as Mary did not hear the complaints. To those who say these things, our Lord will answer them. If things continue to be well with those who say and think such things against us, then so be it. Yet most often, within a few days, despite their efforts to scheme against us with their words and their thoughts, they will be shamed.

The Lord will answer for us in the spirit. God will steer others in the same spirit to give us the things that we need in this life, be it food or clothes or whatever our need is. God sees to these details as we show we will not leave this labor of love for the worries of the world. This may lead to a confusion of error for worldly people who say that it should not be lawful for people to set themselves apart to serve God in the Contemplative life unless they have first secured their bodily needs. These are the same ones who say things like: "God sends that cow but does not deliver it," implying that God does not supply needs until one meets God half way. Truly, they speak these things wrongly of God. Rather, to those who trust steadfastly, God will send what is needed, without need for worry. God will meet us with the necessities, both in strength of body and in the patience of the spirit, for those who bear the need. What else is there that one would need? For all things necessary will come to those who are Contemplatives.

Regarding those who would have doubts that God will do this, the devil is in their heart and robs them of their faith in what they ought to believe. They have not yet truly turned to God, as they should. It does not matter how fancy they seem to make themselves or how they attempt to show the world who they are; God knows them.

Therefore, those of you who would set off to become Contemplatives as Mary did, who choose to be meek beneath the wonderful height and the worthiness of God, know that God alone is perfect. It is your own wretchedness that is imperfect. Examine yourself to make certain that your special desire to serve is due more to the worthiness of God than to your wretchedness. To those who are perfectly meek, nothing shall be lacking for them, neither in body nor in spirit. For those people who have God, in whom there is plenty enough to meet their needs, they need nothing else in this life.

THE TWENTIETH-FOURTH CHAPTER
Two Loves

The little blind love that we call meekness can only be fully knowable when one is lost within the great Cloud of the Unknowing. In that cloud all other things are put away and forgotten, all virtues are discarded, especially charity.

The purpose of charity is nothing but the way to begin and later to increase your understanding of the love of God. God alone is above all creatures and all humanity, even yourself. This is the rightful work that God has laid before us: to love God Who is above all creation and to love God alone. For the ultimate purpose of this work is nothing else but to produce a bare desire in you that is directed solely toward God. This is a naked desire, not a work of the simple, but the work of a perfect apprenticeship that asks neither a release from pain nor an increase of reward. It is a life directed at nothing but for God alone.

It is true that those committed to God will not look after anything for themselves, whether they are in pain or in bliss, so that God's will would be fulfilled when love is given. It seems that in this work, when God is perfectly loved for God's sake alone, nothing else will suffice. In this work, a perfect worker will not even attempt to endure the thought of anything else that God has made, no matter how holy these thoughts may seem.

There is a second and lower branch of charity where your love for your fellow Christian is truly and perfectly fulfilled. It can be seen by this proof: in this work the truest worker found will have no special beholding to anyone, not even for a sibling or family member, friend or foe! Be one like this: that all who may think of you consider you a sibling and everybody you meet is considered to be part of your family, none more special than any other. All should think of you as a friend and never a foe. Those who think of you will be certain you will never cause them any pain or do any harm in their lives. These will see you as a special friend. In this you are led to them to do as much good as possible, as if each was the best friend that you have ever had.

SECTION IV: The Work

THE TWENTIETH-FIFTH CHAPTER
One Little Act of Love

Again, this is true: you should have no special attachment for anyone in this life, be it friend or foe, sibling or extended family. Such a relationship is not necessary if your commitment to being a Contemplative is perfectly done. As it is with all things under God, everything else must be completely forgotten which does not add to the love that is directed to God. Rather, be virtuous and charitable by the strength of your love for God. Your desires may well grow when you come in contact with common people or as you pray for your fellow Christians, but this is not because of any of your own efforts. Let this be done with no other purpose than to let it be done as a result of your love of God. Let your actions be done speedily as is sometimes needful. True charity asks much, especially when directed to a former foe as well as to your friend, extended family, or your sibling. This love is often directed more to your foe than to your friend.

Nevertheless, in this work you will have no leisure to look after your friends or foes, siblings or anyone in your extended family. In the beginning it is often true that your affection may run more deeply for certain people. It is all right; this is lawful for many reasons. It was with such a deep affection that Christ felt toward John and to Mary and to Peter, and apparently to many others. But in the time, through this work, all are to be loved equally by the Contemplative. Then such a one may feel that love for anyone is caused by no other motive than the desire to love only God. Then all will be loved plainly and nakedly for God's sake, and not your own.

For as all were lost through the sin of Adam, yet all people, through that work which can witness to their wills of the wonder of salvation, have been saved, or can be saved, by the virtue of the Passion found only in Christ.

It is not always in the same manner, but it is often similar to the same manner that a Contemplative who is perfectly affected in this work finds himself/herself united to God in spirit. This is the proof that this work does bear its own witness, doing its work as it strives to show others how to be as perfect as it is itself. For it is true that if a member of the body feels sore, all the other members will likewise be diseased; or if a member is well, all the remaining parts are glad as well. It is right to be spiritually one among all the members of the Holy Church. For Christ is our head and we are the members if we have unity; and those who will be perfect disciples of our Lord can add control of their spirit in this spiritual work.

This work is striving for the salvation of all our brothers and sisters, as our Lord Jesus did with His body on the cross. He did this not for his friends and His brothers and His closest lovers only, but also for everyone, without any special favoritism more to one than to another. All who will leave sin and ask for mercy from God can be saved through the virtue of Christ's Passion.

It is said of this meekness and charity that we can become like this, so it is the most easily understood of all other virtues.

Everything in the world can comprehend God's love, even in this little act of love, as is spoken of now, and as was mentioned before.

THE TWENTY-SIXTH CHAPTER
Salvation for Others

Before you begin to labor after the salvation for others, start your own journey into this high Cloud of Unknowing. Later there will be time for you to rest, but in the beginning you must work. Later it will be necessary for you to labor in the task of showing the path to salvation for others, knowing whosoever will pursue this work must expect trials in this difficult work. This is a truly a difficult task unless the seeker has received the blessing of a very special grace or has, for a long time, already labored in this field.

You must understand the nature of this labor of showing others the way to salvation that you have embarked on. Surely you do not believe it is only a simple devout stirring of love you feel that seems to be continually driving your will to this end; because it is not by yourself that such a calling is made, but it is from the hand of the Almighty God. God is always ready to entrust this work to the soul of one who is inclined to bear such a labor. God seeks the soul who is able to do this work, usually one who has already been doing similar work for a long time.

But do you know what this labor is? Surely this is the work of beating down those internal thoughts that concern us in regard to all creation that God has made. These thoughts hold much power under the Cloud of Forgetting, of which we spoke before.

In all this labor it is only done with the help of the grace of God: this is our labor. The other part of it, the stirring of love that is within you, that is the work of God alone. So go and do your work, confident that God will not fail you.

But act quickly; see how you bear yourself in this labor. See if you are able to stand and abide in yourself! The labor lasts for only a short while, and soon you will be familiar with the greatness and the difficulty of this labor. It may seem difficult and tedious in the beginning before you have developed the necessary devotion and focus; but after you have developed that devotion, it will seem to be a task that is restful, energizing, and light to you. That which may have seemed almost impossible for you to do will soon seem only a minor labor. Eventually you will understand that God sometimes does this work alone, but not always. God works as God likes and God works when the time is right. When God desires to do the work, you will find it wise to leave that work alone. Truly, God doesn't need your help.

Sometimes God will send out a beam of spiritual light that pierces through this Cloud of Unknowing that lies between you and the Godhead. Then, unbidden, you may be shown some of God's private insights of which no one can speak. Then you will feel your affection enflamed with the fire of God's love. More than that I cannot tell you at this time.

That work belongs to God only and without God no one can take it up to speak with anything other than a blabbing tongue. One may wish to speak of such things but dares not. Regarding that work that falls to us to do, when we feel ourselves stirred up and held by God's grace, listen carefully for those words. It is better to heed that calling than to ignore it.

THE TWENTIETH-SEVENTH CHAPTER
Who Will Labor

First and foremost, you who labor for the salvation of others in this work must know when, by what means, and with what discretion you must take in order to labor successfully in it. And who should do this work? The answer is thus: "All who have forsaken the world with a true will, and those who do not seek after the Active life of a Martha, but seek after that life that is called a Contemplative life, as Mary did." This applies to all who would labor in this grace and in this work, no matter who they are, whether they have been habitual sinners or not.

THE TWENTY-EIGHTH CHAPTER
The Work of Salvation

The question of when one should begin to labor in this work of salvation for others has an answer: Not until they, themselves, have cleansed their conscience of those acts of sin which they have beforehand committed, as defined by the common ordinances of the Holy Church.

In order to do the work of salvation for others, such souls must dry up both the root and the ground of their own sins that have always lived within themselves. Confession alone will not accomplish this, no matter how sincere the confession may be. Their sin must be overcome. Therefore, those who are willing to labor in this work must first clean themselves in their consciences. Then, when they have done to themselves what is needful and lawful (in the eyes of the church), let them dispose of those sins boldly and not meekly. They ought to be thankful that they have a deep desire for this cleansing, for this is the work in which a soul needs to labor throughout all one's lifetime. Even if one has never sinned in deed, cleansing is in order.

Until then, even while the souls are dwelling in this deadly flesh, they can see and feel that this human state is an obstruction in the Cloud of Unknowing that lies between themselves and God.

Not only is that true about their own sins, but this pain of the Original Sin will forever be seen and felt among some of God's creation, as can be seen in some of their works. These are works that will forever press in on the mind of the sinner. This state of sin will keep itself between God and the bearer of this pain for as long as is possible.

This Cloud is a righteous act done by God. God had once granted sovereignty and lordship over all creation to humanity. But we allowed ourselves to be willfully stirred by our own sin in that creation and chose to leave the bidding of God, our maker.

Adam could have been fulfilling the bidding of God, but, in his own mind, he felt that all the creatures should be beneath him. As a result of his sin, he found God's creation pressing itself above him, for a time placing itself between the sinner and God. Humanity lost the place it ought to have possessed.

THE TWENTY-NINTH CHAPTER

Who is Saved?

Therefore, anyone who desires to come to that place of cleanliness that was once lost to sin, seeking to win back that innocence that was lost, must rightly expect to labor hard in that task. There will be suffering and pains in it, no matter who that one is, whether a continual sinner or not.

It is hard on all who labor in this work or have attempted it, both those who were sinners and those who were innocents who never sinned greatly. It is by the greater labors that those who have been the greater sinners must labor, even more than those who have sinned little. The task for both is great.

Nevertheless, it happens that some who have been the most horrible and habitual sinners have come to the perfection of this work more quickly than those who have not been such. This is the merciful miracle of our Lord Jesus who grants them grace, to the wonderment of the entire world. For this reason, expect the Day of Judgment to be wonderful, for then all will see the wonder of God clearly and recognize the blessings granted. On that day some who have been most despised and considered to have the least value, worthy of nothing as common sinners, who have been known to be horrible sinners, will be the ones to sit rightfully with the saints in God's sight. Likewise, some who now seem and act so holy and have been considered to be like angels, even some who have never sinned deadly, will sit in full sorrow among hell's damned.

By this you can see that you dare not judge anyone in this life, not even considering what good or evil another has done. It will be only in that final Judgment that all deeds will be fully weighed, but not by humanity's standards regarding whether they are good or evil.

THE THIRTIETH CHAPTER

Judges

When you are asked questions regarding who dares to judge the deeds of others, consider this: Judges in this world are only those who have been given the power and the care over their fellow creatures for a limited time. They judge on standards that are either openly given by the statutes of the laws and the ordinances of the Holy Church, or else privately, as in spirit, at the special stirring of the Holy Spirit, the One to judge in perfect charity. Those who are so chosen ought to be aware that they presume to take upon themselves the judgment of others in regard to blame and reproof for their faults. Unless they truly feel led by the Holy Spirit in this work, knowing that without divine guidance, they who dare to judge will quickly fall into error in their judgments. Therefore, be aware even as you act as judge of yourself, this is a matter between you and your God or between you and your spiritual mentor. But, as regarding the judgment of others, it is best to leave that subject alone.

THE THIRTY-FIRST CHAPTER

Burying Your Thoughts

There will come a time when you feel that you have done all that you can lawfully do to amend yourself to the goals and the judgment of the Holy Church. That will mark the beginning of the time when you ought to begin to labor for the work of the salvation for others. Then it may happen that questionable deeds you have committed previously might return and plant themselves in your mind, pushing themselves in to try to come between you and your God. Perhaps you will find new thoughts or awakenings to other sins within yourself that you had never before considered. You need to forever be faithful and quick to step away from those thoughts with a renewed and fervent stirring of love. Tread down such thoughts beneath your feet.

This is the time when you must endeavor to cover those thoughts and memories with the thickness of the Cloud of Forgetting, burying them so deeply that it is as if you had never possessed such thinking in your life. More so than any other thoughts you have had before, you must bury these new thoughts as soon as they occur. If these thoughts continue to rise up within you, you must put them down again and again, as often as they arise.

Again, as often as they rise, put them down. If you think that this trial is too difficult, you may seek other methods and spiritual means to put those thoughts away from you. Ultimately, you cannot hide them. Only God can reveal to you which methods are best. God has deeper wisdom than you will find in anyone in this life.

THE THIRTY-SECOND CHAPTER

Cowering

To overcome some of these thoughts that trouble you, try these things on yourself and see if you can do better.

Do all you can if you wish that these thoughts would not come so easily and quickly. Dump all thoughts of praise of yourself, for they come between you and your God. God alone is worthy of praise; you are not.

In regard to such thinking, try to simply overlook your thoughts, seeking to fix your mind on things that matter, especially if those other thoughts are of God, even as you find yourself screened from God by that Cloud of Unknowing. If you are able to do this, within a short time you may well be eased of your trials. This trick is easily and truly conceived, for it is nothing but admitting the longing desire for God, to feel and to see God. This desire is an expression of love; it rightfully brings peace to you.

Here is another trick: test yourself with it if you can. When you feel that you cannot put down these thoughts of self-glorification, rather than battle them you should cower before them as a poor and wretched coward would cower when overcome with fear in battle. Do not think that it is folly for you to refuse to strive any longer against these ideas which plague you, but through this cowering you surrender yourself to God's mercy from the hands of your enemy. Do this especially if that enemy is yourself. Then perhaps you can rightfully feel that you have defeated such thoughts. Take care with this trick, for at the proving of this trick you may melt down as ice does to water. Truly, this trick can be cleverly conceived, for it is nothing but the truthful knowing and feeling of yourself as you are, a wretch and a filthy coward, worse than nothing. From this you may come to the sure knowledge and feeling that is the very meekness you desired to find. This meekness is the desire you seek so that God may mightily descend to avenge you from your enemies. God will also take you up and lovingly dry your spiritual eyes, as the father does for his child who was at the point of perishing by the mouths of wild animals but then, at the last instant, was rescued.

THE THIRTY-THIRD CHAPTER

The Burden of Original Sin

At this time there are no more tricks, for you have the grace and the passion to have tried the proof of these techniques that have been given you. In these matters, you ought now to be teaching others. This is as it should be; yet we are all very far from being at that place where we want to be. Perhaps we ought to help others, for in doing this you may be doing it for yourself as well as for them. Teaching is a form of learning.

Continue on, learn and labor quickly in these issues if only for a time. Suffer meekly in the pain and embarrassment; see if you may not soon overcome these self-inflicted flaws. Truly, these flaws can become your own personal purgatory.

Then, your pains will pass and your tricks will have given you over to the God who will graciously accept that offering that is yourself. There is no doubt that you can be cleansed of both sin and the pain of sin. This includes the pain of those special, previously committed sins of your own doing and not the pain of the Original Sin.

As for the pain from the Original Sin, it will be with you always, to the day of your death. No matter how busy you might be in trying to overcome it, it is there. Nevertheless, it should be but a petty annoyance to you, a reward from the pain of your special sins; and yet you will never be without some form of that great travail. For it is out of this Original Sin that there will always spring some new and fresh strains of sin, the type of which you must always strike down, ready to cut it away with that sharp, double-edged, dreadful sword of God's discretion. By this you may see and learn that there is no true security or any real rest in this life.

Nevertheless, a day will come when you will never go back, nor ever again be afraid of your own failings. For it is by grace that you have been able to destroy the pain of your previously committed deeds, as already mentioned. It would be better still if you could become secure in that pain of the Original Sin, or even any new strains of sin that have yet to come. These new sins will inconvenience you but they will do little harm.

SECTION V: Meditations

THE THIRTY-FOURTH CHAPTER

One Way

You are able to come to this work of being a Contemplative only through praying and asking Almighty God for great grace and courtesy by which God will teach you of the Trinity. You do well to learn these things. This is a work that God alone can accomplish, and it is especially open for those chosen souls, chosen without any deserving or earning on their part. Without this blessing, no one could ever have the wisdom to dream of or desire such a gift.

But our Lord will do this work, as special as it is and as often as it is needed. Christ does it especially for those who seek God and He does this more often than we can imagine. The labors we do can only be done through our Lord Who has chosen regular sinners to do God's labor in this world. Christ chooses sinners more often than those who have never greatly grieved Him in comparison to those sinners He calls. God actually calls sinners, intentionally and wisely.

This is something that God does, time and again, for in this God is seen as being merciful and mysterious, beyond our comprehension. God sees that this work is accomplished according to God's will: where and when God wishes.

Yet God does not give this particular grace, nor the labors

found in this work, to any soul who is unable to perform them. There is no soul without grace, nor is there one who is unable to receive this grace. It does not matter whether it is a sinful soul or an innocent soul that God chooses. Grace is given not only to the innocent, nor is it withheld because of sin. To say it is "not withheld" is not to say it is "withdrawn."

Beware of the opportunity for error here, for too often the closer people come to touching upon the truth, the more wary they become of error. If you cannot understand what is spoken of here, let it rest until God comes and teaches you these things. Do this, and do not be hurt if you do not understand yet.

Beware of pride, for it is a blasphemy to the gifts of God and it makes sinners bolder than they ought to be. Those who are meek will understand this word: God gives grace freely without anyone deserving it or earning it. The nature of meekness is such that only its very presence within you enables your soul to have it and to feel it. The nature of this is so important that no soul has the ability to become a Contemplative without this grace. This is a part of the calling we receive to come to this labor, without any thought of ever leaving it. This is because anyone who feels this calling will be able to accomplish it and nothing more. It is true: without this calling from God, the soul can neither covet it nor even know to desire it. No matter how much you wish for it and desire it, or no matter how much of it you have, either more or no less, there can be no will or desire for a thing you never knew to desire. God alone can stir you to wish and desire such a thing, even if you never knew you wanted it. Therefore be at peace, for you never need to desire more. Instead, go forth always and do those good things you have already been doing.

If you allow those things that you are already doing to lead you where they will, you will soon understand. Be the laborer and be the sufferer; do look upon your life to judge yourself, but leave it alone. Do not meddle with these things as if you might help them develop lest you spoil it all. You are only the tree; you must trust the millwright to make lumber out of you. You are only the house; you must allow freedom to those living within you. Be like one who is blind for now. Steer away from the covetousness of knowing, for the desire to know more will hinder you rather than help you. It is enough that you feel yourself stirred with these things that you can never fully understand. Be content to always possess those stirrings of heart. It will lead you to have no special thoughts for anything but God, and so intentionally that one day you can come as one unashamedly naked before God with nothing to hide.

If it can be so, then I urge you to trust fully only in the God Who stirs your will and your desires, plainly onto God alone and without having any other motive on God's part or on your part. Do not be afraid of the devil in these matters, for the evil one will not come close. The devil is generally unable to stir someone's will, although occasionally and by some strange means Satan has done even that. But it may have been done by this devil who is not a very subtle devil. Keep you eyes on God and you will do well. It is also true that a good angel can't stir your will either; no, nothing and no one but God alone can do this.

May these words offer you some understanding of what has been said—but even more clearly may you see the proof—that in this work we have no part. Without the call and grace of God, others will not come to this place we desire. All good things depend upon that grace and there is no other means. There is no other way that can lead you there.

THE THIRTY-FIFTH CHAPTER

Lessons, Meditations, and Prayers

Grace is the only way to Salvation. However, there are other things with which a Contemplative apprentice ought to be occupied, especially those involving their Lessons, Meditations, and Prayers. Another way to look at these three might be to call them Reading, Thinking, and Praying. Of these three matters, you can find they are adequately written about in the books of others who are able to state these things much better than this book can, so there is no need to speak to you of these qualities. But this we know: these three concepts are coupled together. Absolutely anyone who wishes to profit from them may do so, their reward is not only given to those who are walking along on that path to perfection but is open to all.

However, do note that thinking alone may not be a good thing without the reading and hearing about those things that have come beforehand. Please understand this: reading and hearing are generally the same. As church clerics can read the books, so do common people read the clerics when they hear them preach the Word of God. No prayer can be as good for beginners or as proficient for them without there having been some history regarding these things that had happened beforehand. Seek, for these proofs are found in other books.

God's word, whether written or spoken, is like a mirror. Spiritually, the eye of your soul is your reasoning just as your conscience is your spiritual image. It is as if you had a spot of dirt on your face; your eye will not see that spot nor know where to look without a mirror to see yourself. Spiritually, this mirror can be like the teachings of others. Without reading or hearing God's Word, it is not possible for anyone to understand that a soul, blinded by its familiarity to sin, could not see a foul spot in its own conscience until its true reflection is shown.

This happens when one looks into a mirror, at either the flesh or spirit, or learns by the teachings from another. Then they may learn of the foul spots in their image. Be it either the flesh or the spirit, only when they learn of the spot will they know to run to the water to wash themselves clean. If this spot is any special sin, then they ought to seek the holy water of the Church, the waters of confession with all its benefits and costs. If the sins are blindly rooted and cause an awakening of sin, then it is to these holy waters of the most merciful God that one must turn. This is the water of prayer with all its benefits and costs.

So it is that you may see that no one's thinking can be good if it stands alone in the dark. This is true for either those who are beginners as well as for those already proficient at thinking. Without previous reading or hearing to prepare one, there can be no prayer that occurs without thinking.

THE THIRTY-SIXTH CHAPTER

Words

This idea, that there can be no meaningful prayer without thinking, may not necessarily be recognized by those who continually labor in the work of this book. From their own meditations, they may have sudden understanding about blind feelings regarding their own wretchedness as well as a sense of awe for the goodness of God. All this may have been achieved without any previous reading or hearing, or without any special regard for anything of God. Sudden insights and blind feelings may well have been lessons from God and not learned from others. There are some things earthly teachers cannot teach you.

At this time there are no further demands on you if you have no meditations other than those on your own wretchedness and of the goodness of God. This is true only if you feel yourself being stirred by either grace or by counsel. In your meditations you need to have a special regard for the words like SIN or GOD, or any other particular words that you alone might consider. Do not be overly profound in your definitions. Do not define or expound upon these words with great subtlety of mind regarding the qualities of these words lest you manipulate their meanings. It is understandable that you might be tempted to do so in an attempt to seemingly increase your devotions. Let it never be so. Find special words and hold them as deep words beyond your understanding.

Hold SIN as if it were a lump that you never will understand, as you should regard any of the things about yourself. There is a blind beholding of sin concealed in this lump (knowing this lump is nothing other than yourself). There is no need to tie any such obligation to yourself at this time except this: that whoever looks upon you should think you are fully sober in your body. Be without any fluctuation of countenance whether you are sitting or going, lying or leaning, standing or kneeling, or even when you are at rest.

THE THIRTY-SEVENTH CHAPTER

One Word

It is right for those who seek to be Contemplatives to purposely meditate as they continuously labor, never forgetting that grace which enables them to work. They should pray whenever it seems they should do so, even if the urge comes suddenly and without any reason. The prayers of such persons are righteous. Here we speak of their special prayers and not merely those prayers that have been ordained by the Church. For those who are true laborers in this course of work often do not bother to use worship prayers outside of church. They are free to pray in the form and statute as they have been taught by the Holy Fathers before us or as they are so led. Their special prayers rise suddenly to God without any special means or premeditation coming either before or after them.

If their prayers are offered in words, as they seldom are, then it is best if they use only a few words. Truly, the fewer words the better. If their prayer can be reduced to only a single word of one syllable, it is better than a word of two syllables. This is in accordance with the work of the Holy Spirit; those who spiritually labor in this work should always be at the highest and most sovereign point of the Spirit.

This can be seen in the following example: A man or a woman may live in the fear of fire, or of death, or whatever else their fear might be. Suddenly, in their spirit, they are drawn, quickly and urgently, to cry or pray for help. Look, see how earnestly they pray! They do not use many words, hardly do they pray in a word of two syllables. And why is that? For they think there is no time to delay, that there is not enough time to declare the exact nature of their needs and the work of their spirit. So they burst out loudly with a great spirit, and they cry but a single word of one syllable, even if the word was "Fire!" or "Help!"

A powerful little word like "Fire!" stirs and pierces the ear of all who hear. It evokes a response. So, too, does a prayer of one little word of one syllable, especially when it is not merely spoken or thought but is emotionally driven from the depth of the spirit. Such a cry made from the depth of heart might be described as being from the heights, for in spirituality all are one, height and depth, length and breadth. Thus, a single, small word pierces the ear of Almighty God more than does any long Psalter unmindfully mumbled in the mouth. This is the reason it is said that a short prayer pierces heaven most quickly.

THE THIRTY-EIGHTH CHAPTER

Height, Depth, Breadth, Length

How can this sort of prayer pierce heaven with only a short word of one syllable offered in prayer? Because it can be prayed with a full spirit, offered from the utmost height and depth, length and breadth of our spirit as it is prayed. It is offered from this height because it can be expressed with all the might of the spirit. Long sentences get bogged down. It is the simple word that has a depth of truth, for a little syllable can better contain the weight of our spirit. As for length, it feels its loneliness and cries out in its loneliness. Likewise, in its breadth it desires the same for all others, even as it wishes these things for itself. In this way it is something only a soul can comprehend, a message fit for heaven.

As we have seen in the lessons of Saint Paul, as with all the saints, not fully but only in a partial manner, we pray in accordance to this work. This is the length and the breadth, the height and the depth of the Everlasting and All-loving, Almighty and All-wise God. The everlastingness of God is Length, God's love is Breadth, God's might is Height, and God's wisdom is Depth.

It is no wonder then that a soul can be nearly conformed by grace to the image and the likeness of God, our maker.

Again, the shortest of prayers is the one that is most quickly heard by God. This is so, even if it is from a frightfully sinful soul, one who has been an enemy to God. When it comes, through grace, to cry such a lone syllable from the height and the depth, the length and the breadth of his spirit, it is heard. Even a desperate sinner, despite the hideous nature of this cry, would always be heard and helped by God.

Consider this example: Think of one who is your deadly enemy, yet when you hear that one's voice cry out in fear from the depth of spirit, yelling one little word such as, "Fire," or this single word, "Help," you react without any consideration of the fact that such a one is your enemy, but from the pure pity in your heart, find you must help. You discover that within you is stirred a pity and find there, residing within you, a kinship resulting from the grievous nature of that deep cry. Without thought, you find yourself assisting your enemy in need. Even if it is a midwinter night, you will help to quench the fire, to calm and comfort your enemy who is in distress.

A compassionate soul is made to be merciful through grace, to have much mercy and pity on one's enemy, regardless of past enmity. In a similar way, think of what pity and what mercy God will have for the spiritual cry of a soul when it is made and wrought from the height and the depths, the length and the breadth of God's spirit. Consider the kindness that we receive by grace. Surely, without comparison, such a one who has received this blessing from another who had once been considered foolish or wicked will have more mercy in the future. This is a thing that is made with kindness. Consider these things; they are had by grace.

THE THIRTY-NINTH CHAPTER

The Single Word

It is good to pray from this height and this depth, this length and this breadth of spirit. Again, you do not need to use many words, not if a single word of one syllable will suffice.

What will this word of your choosing be? It certainly must be a word best suited according to the properties of your prayer. And what word is that? The proper prayer word is the single word that you can understand most clearly. It is the word that will best suit your prayerful purposes.

Prayer in itself, when properly motivated, is nothing but a devout intent directed towards God, either for gaining some good or for removing of some evil.

Be careful when you pray, for it is true that all evil can be comprehended in the concept of sin, either through its cause or by its existence. So when we intently pray for the removal of evil, neither say nor think nor mean anything else, keeping it simple. Use no other words than this one little word, "SIN." Do not dwell on the meaning of your sins, but merely on the word.

Likewise, if you intently pray for the getting of a good blessing, cry out, without any other word or thought or desire, nothing else, and say no more than this single word, "GOD." It is in God that all goodness can be found, both in cause and in purpose.

You should have no surprise if you find you have set these two words ahead of all others. There are many short words, yet none are as fully comprehending of God in the range of all that is good and all that is evil as these two words cover. If anyone has been taught by God to take any other words, take them and leave these two words behind. Do so quickly. But do not study, seeking better words, for by doing so you will never come to the purpose of this work. True learning and real grace are never acquired by study, but only by grace. Therefore, again, seek for no other words with which to pray, but take those words for yourself as you are stirred by God to take. If God stirs you to use these, never leave them. Pray in those God-chosen words and nothing else. And when you pray, why should they not be short words?

Understand this, although the shortness of prayer is greatly recommended here, nevertheless, the frequency of prayer is never limited. For as it has been said before, prayer is to be prayed at whatever length and in however deep the sense of spirit is. It should never cease until that time when it has been fully satisfied with that for which it was longingly prayed. Recall the example used of a man or woman who lived in fear, as was spoken of before. They should never cease crying out this little word "Help," or this little word, "Fire," until that time when they have found help to save them from their anguish.

THE FORTIETH CHAPTER

Both Words

In this same manner, fill your spirit with the spiritual meaning of the word "SIN" without any consideration as to what kind of sin you are considering, be it minor or deadly; be it pride, wrath, envy, covetousness, slothfulness, gluttony, or lechery. What do you think the Contemplative's view of sin really is, or how great a sin it might be? When Contemplatives think of sin, they think of all sin wrapped up in one word: SIN. They consider each sin as being great in and of itself. This is because even the slightest sin would lead them away from God and leave them with no spiritual peace.

Learn to feel that all sin is but a lump. You may never know what the real substance of sin is; however, most often it is nothing other than yourself. For this reason we ought to cry out spiritually, always crying: "Sin, sin, sin! Help, help, help!"

This is a spiritual cry better taught to us by God than by the worldly proofs so readily given you by those around you. This is the cry that is best offered with a pure spirit, without special thoughts, or the pronouncing of any special, formulated words. It will be a rare time when, for the abundance of spirit, it breaks forth into words so strong that the body and the soul will both be filled with sorrow and encumbered with sin.

In the same way and in a like manner, you should use this other little word, "GOD." Fill your spirit with the spiritual meaning of it without any special consideration to any of God's works. Do not consider whether this word is good, better, or altogether the best, not even whether it is meant to be a physical or spiritual word. There is no virtue that will be worked in one's soul without God's grace. Do not be concerned whether these words contain meekness or charity, patience, abstinence, hope, faith, soberness, chastity or willful poverty, or even if they will help or hinder you. None of these words should ever touch the Contemplatives, even though they may feel that they are all virtues from God. The truth is these words will tell you that in God is everything, both in cause and in purpose. If you hold these words and thoughts too preciously, they will have you think that in having them you have God. You do not have God.

Again, do not hold these words too preciously, they may sway you into believing that you already have all that is good and you are without need to covet anything special, that you should be content with the goodness that only God possesses. In the same way, do not think you are going forth in this grace that is found in God only, and completely in God.

To the Contemplative, there should be nothing in either your mind or your will but God alone!

Yet please understand this, that while you live your life in this wretched world, you will always feel, in some way, the burden of this foul stinking lump of sin. It is as if it were united and congealed with the very substance of your own being. Therefore, it is wise if you alternatively weigh only these two words—SIN and GOD. As you do so, consider this thought: that if you have God, then you should lack sin; while if you lack sin, then you should have God.

THE FORTY-FIRST CHAPTER

In Sickness and in Health

An important question is to ask what sorts of discretion do you need in order to become a Contemplative? The answer is simply: "None!" In all the things you do, you should have discretion in eating, in drinking, in sleeping, in the keeping of your body from bitter cold or heat, in long praying or reading, in talking with your fellow Christian, and in all you do. In these things you need to remain discrete so that they will never become either too great a burden for you or too little. But in this work of which we now speak, you have no real way to evaluate the sort of discretion you need. Yet, you cannot cease from this vigilance as long as you live.

This is not to say that you will be able to continue in this work forever without growing weary; that cannot be. At times sickness or some other unexpected affliction will come to your body and soul, as well as other kinds of problems that will appear and deeply afflict you. These pains and woes will try to drag you down from the intended spiritual heights of your labors. You will always have them, be they in earnestness or in folly; meaning, you will have them in all you do. For the sake of God's love, you must be as aware of your work in times of sickness as you are when you are in good health. You ought never be the cause of your own feebleness, as you may be tempted to claim. Truly, this work demands much perseverance, as well as a wholesome and clean disposition, both in your body and soul.

Let God's love govern you discreetly in your body and soul, keeping you in good health as much as possible. If sickness does come to you, have patience and wait for the application of God's mercy; and all will be good enough. There is a trial of patience in any sickness, as there are with other kinds of tribulations. It pleases God greatly, and does so more than any other similar devotion as you show yourself to be faithful in times of your trials. It is a good thing. This is even true but less obvious in the times of your good health.

THE FORTY-SECOND CHAPTER

Self-Control

How do you govern yourself discretely in matters of necessity, in diet and sleep and all the manner of things? Briefly stated, "Take only that which you can get simply." Do this without ceasing from your work and without displays of obvious discretion. Do this and you will come to perform your labors without heavy consideration, understanding that you may find you can cease from some of your other works without great dismay. A soul that continues in this work night and day, purely and without this self-limiting discretion, would never err into those ways that are overtly outward and evil; yet even those people who limit themselves will always have to fight sin.

You need to experience an awakening to fully understand this spiritual work within your soul. Then you must crush any reckless desire in your eating and drinking, in sleeping and speaking, and in all your outward doings. Discretion in these things is better than reckless behavior caused by reasoning or trying to justify these things. You will be a witness to that goal, even as you measure it by those standards by which all things are measured. You should never be the cause of awakening sins in yourself or in others, not by any means.

Let the people say what they will say, but let the proof of these things be its own witness. Therefore, lift up your heart to a blind stirring of love. Know what you mean when you say SIN and what you mean when you say GOD. It is GOD you should have, and SIN you should lack. Yet, although God wants you, it is SIN of which you can be most certain. Now, in this matter, may the goodness of God help you, for now is the time when you have need of this witnessing word!

THE FORTY-THIRD CHAPTER

Forgetting Yourself

Look to make sure that nothing is at work in either your mind or your will except God alone. Refrain from thinking and feeling any of those things that could be less than God, losing such thoughts completely in that Cloud of Forgetting.

You must understand that in this work, in this Cloud of Forgetting, you need to forget everything in God's creation other than yourself, forgetting their deeds as well as your own. In this work you will eventually forget even yourself and the deeds you have done for God's sake, as well as all of creation and its deeds. Be in the condition of the perfect lover who not only loves the object of this passion more than such a one loves the self, but also hates the self for the sake of that very thing that is loved most.

This is what you are to do with yourself. You must come to loathe and be wary of all these things that are at work in your mind and will, driving them away until only God remains. For what else is there, whatever else could be there, that needs to remain between you and your God? It is no wonder then that you would come to loath yourself and even hate to think of yourself when you realize that this self is sinful, which it is. It is only a foul and stinking lump that you will never know regarding its exact nature. If you did not reject it but allowed it to remain, it would reside between you and your God.

Again, this lump of sin is nothing other than yourself. You must understand that it is only a united and congealed mass made of the substance of your sinful being. It desires to remain within you; it has no desire to depart from you.

Therefore, you are the one who must break away from all thinking and feeling for everything in God's creation, but mostly from yourself. For it is only in this kind of thinking and feeling for yourself where you are able to leave your thinking and feeling for all creation. In truth, when compared to your thoughts of yourself, all God's creation can be lightly regarded. For, and you can best use yourself to be the proof of this, you will find when you have forgotten all other creatures and all their works, and even your own works, or anything that would lie between you and your God, you have forgotten nothing that was good. To recognize this is to expose your thinking and feelings about your own being and worth. Then, even this thinking and feeling always needs to be destroyed if you ever truly want to feel the perfection of this work.

THE FORTY-FOURTH CHAPTER

Love and Sorrow

How can you destroy these thoughts and feelings that exist within your own self? Their destruction would make you vulnerable. Do you think that these thoughts can be destroyed as all other hindrances were destroyed? You are correct in this. But without the full and special grace of God, freely given and in full accordance with your ability to receive this grace, these exposed thoughts and feelings can never be destroyed.

The ability to receive this grace is nothing less, and requires nothing more, than a strong and deep spiritual sorrow. In this sorrow you need to have discretion to understand these matters. You must always be carefully aware that, during any time of sorrow, you do not put too harsh a strain on either your body or your spirit. Learn how to sit still, as if you were in a deep sleep, exhausted from your weeping, sunk deeply in your sorrow. This is true sorrow; this is a perfect expression of that sadness, and it is good for one to know the depths one can sink in one's own sorrow.

All people know sorrow, but those who feel it especially deeply are those who know the depth of their own sorrow. In this they know themselves and their feelings better. In comparison, all other sorrows will prove to be shallow. But those who take this true sorrow onto themselves will discover how deeply they are truly corrupted. These are the ones who know real sorrow. Those who have never felt this depth of sorrow, although they may seem sorrowful, have not felt perfect sorrow.

Sorrow, when it is found, cleanses the soul not only of sin, but also of the pain that has been earned by sin. This is what makes a soul able to receive this newfound joy, the joy that can distract a soul from thinking and feeling about the depth of its sadness. This sorrow, if it is truly conceived, is a holy desire. If it is not real, it will never lead a person who dwells in this world to live on a higher plane while being able to bear that truth.

A soul is not rewarded with comfort in return for its righteous workings. If it were it would never be able to bear any pain regarding either its thinking or feeling in its search for the truth. For as often as such a one would approach honest thinking and feeling toward God with innocence and purity of spirit, as it may be the case with you, such a person will quickly come to feel that this could not possibly be the case. Such people always find their thoughts and feelings occupied and filled with ideas from that foul and stinking lump which can only be themselves.

These are the very things that need to be forever hated, despised, and forsaken if that person expects to ever be a perfect disciple of God. These are things that are learned regarding oneself on the mountain of perfection. Some people seem to go mad from the sorrow, in so much that they weep and wail, struggle, curse, and swear until they think they bear too heavy a burden upon themselves, that they can never find anything of value within themselves. It is here when God is well pleased, for then we are most vulnerable.

For in all this sorrow, the seeking soul must never desire to cease this existence or to avoid the pain, for that would be to the devil's joy and an insult to God. The one who listens rightly may well know, when heartily thanking God for the worthiness and the gift of God's being, that all that is truly desired is to stop thinking and feeling about one's own existence.

To the souls who have borne this sorrow and felt these pains, these sorrows and desires become, in one way or another, tools by which God gives them the spiritual growth to be disciples. This willingness is in accordance to the ability of the body and soul, in both degree and complexion, until that time when they can move perfectly to be united with God in perfect love—as God wills it.

THE FORTY-FIFTH CHAPTER

Falseness

From now on, there is nothing about this work that will help a young disciple who has not yet been well tried and been proven in spiritual workings. Unless and until one has endured trials, one can be easily deceived. Untried young disciples will soon be at war within themselves. They need the grace to cease from that war. They need to seek counsel before they are destroyed in their flesh, falling into those fantasies of their spiritual minds. All of these troubles are the result of the desires of pride and flesh and curiosity of intelligence.

This is how those who are new can be easily deceived and fall. A young man or young woman, seeking after a clear picture of devotion, will hear of the sorrowful stories and frustrated desires endured as such stories are read and discussed by elders. They may wonder how such people dare to lift up their hearts unto God with unceasing desires to feel that love of God if only pain and sorrow follow. As quickly as their curiosity is aroused, they begin to conceive that these words could not be spiritual as they were meant to be, but that it is some sort of a trial for the new members. It will sound to them that they are expected to put a fleshly and bodily flavor to these tales until they, the newest members, begin floundering in the fleshly desires of their hearts. It sounds as if, with their lack of grace, they deserve such a fate as is befitting all who carry pride and curiosity within themselves. They may well strain their veins and bodies in a most beastly and rude manner trying to accomplish a state they are still incapable of achieving. In a short time they fall out of faith into worries, adopting a manner of listless feebleness in body and in soul. This is the same behavior which makes them lose their way, enabling them to seek an easier but false manner of fleshly and bodily living with comforts elsewhere. They make it seem as though they thought all things were only for the recreation of their body and the spirit.

Or else, they may fall into another kind of trap, snared because of their spiritual blindness and inflamed flesh, victims of the temperament they often carry within themselves. Their devotion is too often only a feigned fleshly nature and not a spiritual working. They have allowed their hearts to be enflamed with an unkindly heat of complexion, caused both by the misuse of their bodies or by this feigned working. Often they conceive this false heat to be wrought by the devil, that fiend that is their spiritual enemy, when, in truth, the falseness is caused by their own pride on account of their fleshly desires and their mental curiosity.

Still worse, proceeding further away from God, they may imagine this to be God's fair offering of love to them, something kindled by the grace and the goodness of the Holy Spirit. Truly, of this deceit and of the branches thereof, there springs forth great damage in many forms of hypocrisy with much heresy and many errors. For quickly after such a false feeling comes, there also comes a false knowing that is from the fiend's school. It comes as certainly as what follows after the true feelings from a true knowledge of God's school. Be very careful; the devil has his contemplatives as surely as God does. This deceit of false feelings and false knowledge that follows after every new member has many wondrous variations, for of such are the diversities of state and the subtle conditions that follow the one who has been deceived. This is as sure as the true feeling and knowledge of the one who has been saved.

But when one becomes a Contemplative, no more deceits come except those by which you know will soon be assailing you if you purpose to labor in this work. For what good would it profit you to consider how these great scholars, as well as men and women of degree other than yourself, have been deceived? Surely, nothing good would come from it. You need to know nothing more except to know that things will fall on you if you continue in this work. You must be wary in all your labors, for you will be assaulted there.

THE FORTY-SIXTH CHAPTER

Heed not your own Heart

For your sake and for the sake of God's love, be wary. In this work, do not overstrain your heart too much. Work more with passion than with brute strength. Yet always be in a desire with some longing, meekly and spiritually, otherwise your work may become crude, both worldly and fleshly. Therefore, hear these words again: Be wary.

Surely, no beastly heart dares to presume to touch the high mountain of this work, but it ought to be driven away with stones. Stones, by nature, are hard and dry and hurt when they hit their target. Truly, such rude longings to "touch the mountain" of God have been formed in fleshly ways of the body's desires, but these feelings are dry from not knowing grace. These dry feelings may be fully capable of hurting the simple soul, leaving it in festering pain that was begun as a fantasy feigned by fiends. Beware of this countenance, whether in body or in soul. Instead of giving it heed, learn to love in courtesy and in meekness and trust the will of our Lord. Grasp not at those things of God as if you were a greedy greyhound, pretending to suffer with a hunger you've never known. Do things in your way, but refrain from listening to the crude and the deep stirring of your spirit. There is also wisdom in keeping these desires of your heart from God, to keep from God the depth of your desire to please and serve God alone.

This probably sounds as if it is childishly and playfully spoken,; but whoever has the grace to do and feel these things is one who could find joy in this playful work with God that the world cannot understand. These of the world act as if they do not know God is the Father who loves each and all the children, kissing and holding them to show that all is well.

THE FORTY-SEVENTH CHAPTER

Things Kept from God

Perhaps this sounds like you were being treated as if you were a child in this matter, making it sound like folly, as if you lacked any kind of discretion in understanding the message of this book. But there is an element of truth and knowledge regarding these things that, if you were not told, might cause you to wrestle for a long time before you began to understand them. These things are spoken for your sake.

There is a reason why you should hide the deep desires of your heart, this passion you have for God. In this matter, may your understanding come clearer regarding the knowledge of God you seek, thereby increasing your chances of fulfilling your desires. By hiding your passion to serve only God, it may reveal the truth and the depth of that desire more clearly than by any other method you might employ.

There is another reason for this; for by such a hidden display, you may bring yourself away from any reckless ways that your fleshly feelings might lead you and, instead, have them lead you into the purest and deepest of spiritual feelings. Thus, in the end, it will help you to tie that spiritual knot of love between you and your God, in spiritual unity in accordance to God's will.

You would do well to consider this, for God is a spirit and whoever should be dedicated to God is to be united in truth and depth of spirit, far from any feigned fleshly expressions of devotion. While it is true that all things are known to God and nothing can be hidden from God's knowing, neither fleshly nor spiritual things, there is an even more open way than what God's knowing has shown. That is hidden in the depth of spirit. Since God is a spirit, there is nothing that is mixed with any manner of the flesh that can bother God. All things of the flesh are things that lead us further from God, following a course of our nature rather than those spiritual things. By this reasoning, it seems that while our desires are mixed with all kinds of worldliness, it is by this thinking that we cause ourselves stress and strain in trying to live both in the spirit and the body together. As long as anything moves us further from God, even if it is done devoutly and eagerly in soberness, in purity, and in the depth of spirit, it is wrong.

Here again you may see some of the reason why you are urged to be childlike, concealing the very stirrings of your desire for God. You should not playfully hide it; this would be the behavior of a fool. In a spirit of lightness, this should not be done. Rather, do that thing within yourself which seems right: hide those feelings from God and the world and yourself. It is better if you would cast that truth into the depths of your spirit, far from the crude meddling of anything fleshly. This kind of fleshly interference is capable of making you less spiritual and can move you further from God. The more your spirit has spirituality, the less it has of the flesh and nearer it is to God. This does please God and is clearly seen time after time. This is not to imply that

God's sight may be, at any time or in any manner, clearer than at any other time; for God's wisdom and eyesight is evermore unchangeable. This manner of behavior is more like what God expects. Remember, God is in the purity of spirit because God is spirit.

There is another reason for you to keep this desire to yourself and not let God know of it, and that is because you are, as well as many others such as ourselves, able to comprehend this: a spiritual thing is as if it were a fleshly thing. It is for this reason that you don't show God the very stirrings of your heart. If you do this, you might show a desire of the flesh, both in countenance and in voice. Your words might show some crude fleshly straining as is revealed when you would show a secret thing that is hidden in your heart that is only a heart of flesh. If this were true, then your work would be impure. For in this manner, such a thing can be shown to others, and there is another way in which it can be shown to God.

THE FORTY-EIGHTH CHAPTER

Thoughts

You should never cease your work. If you are stirred to pray with your mouth or to burst out with words caused by an abundance of your spiritual devotion that makes you speak to God or to people, I urge you to speak the good words as you feel yourself led to speak. But let it be words and simple phrases like these: "Good Jesus! Fair Jesus! Sweet Jesus!" It might be better if God would forbid you from behaving thus, but God will do and bid what God will. God forbid that we should ever separate what God has brought together, the body and the spirit. For God will be served with both body and soul, together, it seems. God will reward the one who serves with a reward that is blissfulness to both the body and in the soul.

In all aspects of this reward, sometimes God will passionately reward a devoted servant in this lifetime, not only once or twice, but often, as God wishes, with wonderful sweetness of comforts. Of these rewards, they do not come from the world into the body, but they come from within the body. These rewards come from the windows of our minds, from within that blessed servant, rising and springing forth in the abundance of spiritual gladness and of true devotion in the spirit. Others should not hold such a reward of comfort and sweetness in suspicion. Those who know such rewards have no doubt about the source from Whom the blessings come.

But of the other comforts that may come to you, whether they are sounds or gladness or sweetness, comforts that suddenly come from the world that you never know where they come from, I urge you to hold them with suspicion. They may be good or evil: if they are of a good angel, they are good; but if they are of an evil angel, they are evil. This is true: they will not be evil if their deceits do not lead you astray in your natural curiosity or the unnatural desires of your fleshly heart. You must learn to discriminate. If this comfort they offer does not lead you astray and is not the cause of this discomfort, meaning a devoted stirring of love, it comes from the spirit of purity. This, then, is from the hand of the Almighty God without a doubt. It is proper for us to always to be far from any fantasy of the mind or any false opinion that might easily beguile us in this life.

Of the other comforts and songs and sweetness, how can you know whether they are good or evil? You can find this wisdom of discernment written in other places and in the works of others, said a thousand times better than could be said or written here. Seek for it there, not here.

Do not be hindered; do not push yourself to find wisdom in this world. Instead, fulfill the desire and pursue the stirring of your heart concerning those graces that you have shown in yourself to possess before this time, both through your words and your deeds.

But this can be said to you regarding the sweetness of those things that enter through the windows of your own mind, things that will be both good and evil. You must make continual use of your blind, devout, and eager stirring of love to discern their nature, the sort of discernment of which you have often read about in these pages. With time and experience, it will be easier for you to sort them out as to whether they are good or evil. Yet it may happen that they sometimes astonish you at your first encounter with them, but that is only because they are strange and uncouth. They will do to you what they can, enticing your heart so fast that you may not be able to give them the full and careful examination that you should. At that time, you may need to have them certified by the wonderful spirit of God or else judged by the counsel of some discreet mentor.

THE FORTY-NINTH CHAPTER

Perfection of Will

You must prayerfully and eagerly lean upon that meek stirring of love that is in your heart and follow after it. This will be your guide in life and it will bring you to a spiritual joy in the life to follow. This is the substance of all good living; without it no good work may be begun or ended. This is nothing but the good and conforming will toward God. It is the source of the satisfaction and gladness that you find in your heart; it is the joy you feel for all that God does.

This is the good will that is the substance of perfection. All the sweetness and comforts, whether in the body or in the spirit, when compared to this, seem to be only accidental, no matter how holy they may seem to others. Nothing else can hamper this good will. The world calls them accidents, but you may either have them or lack them and you would be missing nothing. I speak here only of things in this life, but it will not be so in the bliss of heaven. In heaven they will be united with that substance of perfection without fail, as it shall be in the body as it is with the soul. The substance of them here is only a good spiritual will. When one feels the perfection of will, as it may be known in this life, there can be no other sweetness or comfort that can appeal to anyone here. If you do not feel this comfort, you will be neither glad nor sad to lack it, knowing it is given for the sake of God's will.

THE FIFTIETH CHAPTER

Both the Weak and Strong

By this you can see that you should direct all your focus toward the humble stirrings of love. In all the other sweet offerings and comforts we encounter, be they of the body or spirit, may they never be treated as being more favored or more holy than love. We ought to treat all else with a sense of indifference.

As these other things come, welcome them; but do not rely on them lest they weaken you from your true mission, for they can sap your strength if you remain long among their sweet offerings. Beware so that you are not stirred to love God for the sake of worldly rewards and comforts. If you begin to feel that way, you will greatly resent it when they are taken away. If that is possible, you will know your love is not yet chaste or perfect. For a love that is chaste and perfect, though it desires that the body be fed and comforted by the presence of such feelings, will feel no resentment for their lack but will probably be pleased to lack them, knowing it is God's will and for your betterment.

Yet it is not uncommon that some live with many comforts, while at the same time others seldom enjoy any such luxuries. But know this: all these things are in accordance to the disposition and the ordinances of God, for God knows what will best profit and serve the needs of all creatures. Some are weak and tender in spirit and they need to be comforted by the presence of such comforts. They could not abide and bear the great diversity of temptations and tribulations that they might have otherwise suffered. They have not the strength to endure the trials in this life against their bodily and spiritual enemies. Some have been so weak in body that they could never manage to do any penance whereby they might cleanse themselves. For these, the Lord will cleanse them fully and graciously in the same spirit with sweet comforting.

But there are also some who, being strong in spirit, can find their own comforts within their own souls. These are able to offer up a love that is both reverent and meek, in accordance of will. These are they who do not need to be well fed with sweet comforts in the manner of bodily feelings.

Truly, I do not know which of these is holier and dearer to God, one or the other. Only God knows.

THE FIFTY-FIRST CHAPTER

The Lost One

Through all you endure, you ought to humbly trust this faithful stirring of love in your heart. I do not mean those things that move your fleshly heart, but those that move your spiritual heart, for this is how you find your true will.

Be careful that you do not conceive your own thoughts that are fleshly and choose to think they are spiritual. For truly, the body and the flesh can conceive thoughts that possess temptingly curious and imaginative cravings that can lead you to great error. This is why there is wisdom in hiding your great desire for God within yourself. In the beginning if I asked you to express your desire for God, you may have described it in a more fleshly manner than you would now after it was suggested that you keep that desire hidden. For now you know full well that, when these things are willfully hidden, they are cast to the very depths of the spirit and remain there as a burden for you.

It is for this reason that it is necessary to show great caution when hearing words that are seemingly spoken with a spiritual intent, but that are aimed so you hear them in your flesh and not in your spirit, as they were meant to be heard. It is also good to be aware of the spiritual intent with the words like "IN" or the word "UP", for misunderstanding even these two little words has produced many errors and deceits for those who thought themselves to be spiritual workers. Let us consider some of these deceits, for often there is deceit in the details.

There was a young man, a disciple in God's school, newly turned from the world. When he had given himself over to penance and to prayer for only a short time, he began to listen to his own advice in his own confession. He soon began to think that he was better able to give himself better spiritual instructions than he had heard when others spoke or read aloud. Perhaps he had only read such things to himself. When he had read or heard the spoken words of spiritual workings, especially through his own interpretation, he considered how one might draw all wisdom from within himself. By this he hoped to cause himself to grow more quickly.

With as much blindness in regard to his own soul as well as fleshly curiosity for his own kindled wit, he misunderstood all the words he heard. Next, he found within himself a passion for hidden things, pretending these things he found could be called works of grace. In doing so, he concluded that the counsel that others offered was not in accordance with those things that he felt he should labor toward in his work. Like those others who followed the many false paths, he felt justified in complaining against the counsel of his superiors.

Like all the deluded ones before him, he began to think— yes, and perhaps say to others—that they can find no one who had more wisdom than what he, himself, possessed. He followed the pattern of the lost. As with those who fell away before him, because of the boldness and presumption of their restless imaginations, they quickly left the way of humble prayer and penance and set out on their way (as they imagine it to be) to do the "real" spiritual work as they were directed from within their souls.

His work, though it had been truly and faithfully conceived in his mind, was the work of his flesh and not the work of the spirit. He worked in his own way, and in this he never saw the devil was his chief counsel. This is a quick way to the death of the body and the soul, for it can lead to madness and not to wisdom. He did not know this, for he proposed that any work he did for himself was the same as doing a work for God. He never realized that what he thought was for God really had nothing to do with God.

THE FIFTY-SECOND CHAPTER

Fallen Imagination

Believing in yourself: this is the main way to madness. Those who fall tend to read and hear what is said concerning those things they should be leaving behind. They cherish those old outwardly trappings of their imaginations as they profess to pursue inward works; but soon they grow confused until they do not know which direction to find the inward working. Having listened to themselves and not to the Spirit that would have guided them, they easily begin to labor in the wrong direction. It is far too easy for them to turn their fleshly minds inwardly to satisfy their own bodily comforts even as they turn against the course they had chosen.

They strain themselves until they are convinced they can see better with their fleshly eyes and hear better with their own ears. They continue this process using all of their earthly wits of smell, taste, and inward feelings. In this way, they unwittingly reverse themselves against the course that God would have had them follow and become armed with a new sense of curiosity as they indiscreetly labor in their imaginations. In the end, they have only spun their brains within their skulls. Then, as fast as the devil has power to do so, the evil one will counterfeit some false lights and sounds, bringing sweet smells in their noses and wonderful tastes in their mouths. The devil will do so until there is only a faint trace of quaint hearing of faith. Instead, they burn in their breasts and in their bowels, in their backs and in their kidneys, and in their private members.

And yet, even in this fantasy of their own creation, they think that they possess the true and restful mind of their God without having to let go of their vain thoughts. Surely, they behave in this manner, so filled with falsehood that not even their own vanity can grieve them.

They have encountered that familiar demon that finds them weak, who can minister vain thoughts to them and convince them that they are doing a good thing. He, that same evil one, is the chief laborer of this work.

But you would do well to remember that the evil one does not hinder himself. Regarding the mind of God, the devil would not dare to remove the memory of God completely from those he has seduced. If he did that, he would fear that he would have expose himself to be the one who did this evil.

THE FIFTY-THIRD CHAPTER

The Lost Being Lost

Many wonderful things follow those people who have been persuaded to follow after false works and wandered along other misleading paths. This often seems far more common among the fallen than are found among those who have been God's true disciples. Too often these misled souls seem wonderfully dignified in their appearances, both in the flesh and in the spirit.

But it is not always true with the others who have followed the wrong path. Sometimes you look upon these unfaithful followers as they sit, it seems as if their eyelids were open, staring as if in anger. They have the look of those who had seen the devil. Surely it is good if they are aware of his presence, for in the beginning the fiend is not far away from them. Some of these captives stare with their eyes half-open; as if they were sheep afflicted in the head and now were waiting to die. Some tilt their heads to the side, as if there was a worm in their ear. Some pipe emptiness when they try to speak, it is as if there was no spirit in their bodies. This is the proper condition of the hypocrite. Some cry and whine in their throat, yet they are greedy and hasty in all they say and think. This is the condition of the heretics and of them who are filled with all the presumption and curiosity of mind they can handle. They will always maintain their way of error as righteousness.

Much disorderly and uncomely behavior follows closely after their errors, as is seen when anyone is able to perceive all their actions. Some of these misled souls are eager to keep themselves hidden; thus they can generally refrain from exposing themselves in the company of perceiving witnesses. But if these same souls could be seen when they are in private, these things could not be hidden. Nevertheless, if anyone would openly state an opinion of these misled souls, the truth would burst out in some manner. These people of hidden passions think that all they have to do is proclaim the love of God. They maintain they have the right to speak the only truth they know even when their "truth" is shown to be false.

May God show merciful grace to make them change their ways to that which they once claimed as their love of God, as long and in the same manner before they showed their true selves to be when they ran madly after the devil. The devil has never had such perfect servants in this life as those who have been deceived and infected with all the fantasies spoken of here. You may be certain that some, probably many, have been infected with these things. The devil has no more perfect hypocrite or heretic in his earthly company than those who are guilty, as regarding the things spoken of here, as God permits us to speak.

Some of those who have fallen away are so burdened in their curious behavior regarding their own flesh that, at a time when they ought to be hearing the truth, they quaintly and mockingly shake their heads side to side. With their chins in the air, they gape with their mouths open and tongues protruding as if they were trying to hear with their tongues and not with their ears. Some, when they should be speaking, point with their fingers, stabbing those fingers on their own breasts or on the breast of those against whom they speak. Others cannot sit still, stand still, or lie still unless they are wagging with their head or doing something with their hands. Some row with their arms in tempo as they speak, as if they needed their arms to swim over great waters. Others are forevermore smiling and laughing at each other's words as they speak, being gigglers or foolish jesters or jugglers who lacked any sense. Similarly, there are some others with a sober and demure bearing of body and who seem joyful in their manner.

This is not to say that all their unseemly behaviors are great sins in themselves, nor should all those who do them be considered lost sinners. But if these do seem improper and extraordinary in their manner, let their behavior be the governor of the one who does them. Perhaps they may leave these things that are not of God whenever they wish to. Until then, they have become tokens of pride and the vanity of wit. They reveal an undisciplined showing and display the envy of knowledge. Until they repent, it is especially true that they have become the very tokens of unstableness of their hearts and the restlessness in their minds.

These are the qualities to be avoided. This is the purpose of this book. This is the only purpose as to why so many of these insights have been put down in this writing. This is how spiritual laborers must prove their work.

THE FIFTY-FOURTH CHAPTER

The Contemplative's Demeanor

One thing those who have chosen to become Contemplatives should do is to govern themselves completely and rightly, in the body and soul, thereby making themselves favorably disposed to everyone who might look upon them. This should be true of even the least favored person who chooses to leave the world and come, by grace, to choose this as the labor in which to work. Their countenance should, suddenly and graciously, be so completely changed that each person they meet would be pleased to have them in their company. This is very much the way it should be; that the people they see should be pleased, in spirit and by grace, to feel God in their presence.

Therefore, seek this gift in whatever form this grace may come to you. Those who truly possess this gift know with certainty of their hearts how best to govern themselves and all that belongs to them, for this is the nature of this virtue. They should easily be able to give discretion if there needs to be discernment, of all types and natures. They should know how to make all people like them, whether they were common sinners or not, yet they must be without sin themselves. All who see them may wonder at what they see. In this, they draw others to seek this grace with the same spirit that they saw in those who drew them.

Of those who choose to be Contemplatives, their manner and their words should be full of spiritual wisdom, full of both fire and fruit. When they speak, let it be in solemn truthfulness, without any falsehood, far from any of the fawning or piping of hypocrites.

For again, there are some who, with all of their might, imagine that in their own speaking they actually move to reinforce and support themselves, believing their words are truthful. In this they assume they can prevent themselves from ever falling. With many words of humble piping and images of devotion, careful to look like the image of those enwrapped in holiness, they have witnessed in the sight of all; but they do not consider the view that God and the angels possess of them. Unwittingly, this kind of person will do much to change the truth, making sorrowful patterns for the sake of an unordered image, offering unseemly or unsettling words spoken for the sake of appealing only to our wallets. With their words they offer a thousand vain thoughts and stinking stirrings toward sin that will, in the end, draw themselves to sin as they recklessly expose their emptied selves to the sight of God and the saints and the angels in heaven.

Oh, Lord God, how can this be? How can there be any pride wrapped in meek words of imagined modesty that have been so plentifully spoken? Instead, it should appeal to those who truly are meek in showing their meekness with comely words and faces, according to that meekness that is found within their hearts. It is not to say that the meek should then flaunt themselves with their own shy voices against the plain dispositions of those of their order who seem too readily willing to speak for them and of themselves. If they are true servants, then let them speak in truthfulness and with holiness of voice, for in this their spirit will speak for them. But if one comes to you who speaks with plain words and a simple voice, though that one speaks poorly and yet piping, such a one is likely speaking in the flesh, of things that should remain only between such a one and God or the chosen confessor. Take this to be a token of hypocrisy. Beware: the hypocrites can be young or old, lovely or vile.

We are generally speaking here about venomous deceits. Truly, there are such people. Our prayers should be the sort that, when they are heard, they show grace. True prayer does not leave behind that kind of stench that a hypocrite's words do, prayers that are offered with secret pride in their hearts and lust in their flesh. The false and meek spoken words of the hypocrite will cause many of the poor, unthinking souls to sink into sorrow.

SECTION VII: Directions

THE FIFTY-FIFTH CHAPTER

The Deceiver

The devil deceives unwary people in many manners. He enflames their brains so wonderfully that they will be led to believe that they alone are fit to maintain God's law and they alone are able to reveal or destroy the sin in others. The devil does not have to tempt them with things that are obviously evil; rather he makes them behave like those self-appointed busybodies who vigilantly oversee all the aspects of Christian living in others, just as the abbot does over his monks. They will rebuke all others for their faults as if they had personally been given charge of keeping the souls of others. They think that they can do nothing else, for they believe that they do these things for God's sake. They are quick to tell others of all the faults they see, and then they claim they have been stirred to such action by the fires of charity and by God's love in their hearts. In truth they lie, for it is only the fires of hell welling within their brains and in their imaginations that would make them behave in such a manner.

This is true, as it may be seen in the following example. The devil is a spirit and he possesses no more a worldly body than an angel has. Yet he can take on the form of a body, as an angel does with permission from God. The devil will try to minister to anyone in this world, for this is the evil work that he does. Like angels, the devil's appearance is always in a form that seems to appeal to those he seeks. There are examples of this in the Holy Bible. As angels were sent in the bodily form to the people in either the Old or New Testaments, the form they took was always shown as to what the spiritual nature of the matter or the message was. In the same manner, it is also true with the devil, for when he appears in body, he has some quality of the image within his form that shows his servants the image they desire to see.~

Yet it is also said that whenever the devil takes any bodily form, he also shows some quality in this body that appeals to the spirit of the servants he calls. It is his goal to enflame the imagination of his Contemplatives with the fire of hell, and this he does suddenly and without discretion. Suddenly, curious thoughts appear. Without any consideration of the consequences, the reckless Contemplatives will take it upon themselves to blame others for their own grievous faults. They do this because they have only one spiritual nostril. For that septum, that division that is in the nose to make two nostrils, shows how one must have spiritual discretion, able to discern between the good from the evil. The evil is of the worse part, and the good is of the better part; in this is given the fullness of judgment for anything that one hears or sees done or spoken. By our brains are spiritual things understood and imaginations kindled; by nature this is how it exists and this is how it works in the head.

~A single paragraph, a 182-word section, has been removed from the body of the text and added as an appendix item at the conclusion of the book.

THE FIFTY-SIXTH CHAPTER

The Deceived

There are many who are not deceived by this error as it was set here, yet for the sake of their own pride and natural curiosity for things of intelligence and for their love of the cunningness of words, they choose to leave the common doctrines and counsels of the Holy Church. These, with all their followers, rely heavily on their own knowledge. But since they were never grounded in the humble and blind faith of trust and virtuous living, they deserve to have a false feeling, feigned and wrought by our spiritual enemy. Their rebellion is too much for them to bear until, in the end, they desert and then blaspheme all the saints, sacraments, statutes, and ordinances of the Holy Church. They become the fleshly living ones of the world, the type who think the statutes of the Holy Church are too rigid to be followed. They turn to these heresies quickly and lightly. It is these heresies they faithfully choose to maintain, all the while thinking they can lead their followers to an easier and softer way to heaven than is ordained by the Holy Church.

These are the ones who will not take that straight and narrow way to heaven, going to hell by the soft and easy way instead. People choose their own way. All such heretics and all their followers, if they might see clearly what they will be on the last day, would see they will be fully encumbered by the great and horrible sins of the world. The sins of their foul flesh, done in secret, will be known. They will be openly seen in their plain presumption for maintaining the errors. Then they will be properly called the disciples of the Antichrist. It will be said of them that, for all their false but fair preening in the open, they will be openly known to have been foul lechers in private.

THE FIFTY-SEVENTH CHAPTER

Up

Let us speak no more of evil things at this time, but let us return to that matter of which we spoke earlier: how these young, presumptuous, and spiritual disciples misunderstand another little word: "UP."

For whatever it is that they read, or is read to them, or which they hear spoken regarding how certain others have lifted up their hearts to God, then quickly they begin to stare at the stars as if that would lift them above the moon. They listen in case they can hear angels singing in the heavens. These same souls who sometimes, for the sake of the curiosity of their imaginations, try to pierce the planets or make a hole in the firmament to better understand these things. These are the sorts of people who would make God into the image they wish their God to be. They would clothe their God richly in clothes and set God on the throne far stranger than ever has been depicted in this earth. These self-deluded souls would make angels appear in fleshly images and set them above each one with diverse musical instruments, making them far more curious than was ever seen or heard in this life.

The devil has wonderfully deceived these folks. He will send them a manner of dew, maybe angels' food as they imagine it to be, as if it was coming out of the air, softly and sweetly falling into their mouths. In this manner they are the image of those who sit and gape upward as if they were frogs trying to catch flies. But truly, this showing is only a form of deceit, although some of it may seem to be holy. For those who are so led, in time they will have emptied their souls of any true devotion. There is much vanity and fashion in their hearts that is caused by their strange theology. It is also true that this is often feigned by the devil to be quaint sounds in their ears, quaint lights shining in their eyes, and wonderful smells in their nose. But all of this is falseness.

They who are vulnerable do not believe this, for they think that they have followed the examples of Saint Martin who, in looking upward and watching, by revelation, saw God clad in a mantle among the angels. Again, they think they will see what Saint Stephen saw when he saw our Lord Jesus stand in heaven. They can name others as well, as when Christ, who bodily ascended into heaven, was seen by his disciples. Therefore they insist that we must also lift our eyes up, heavenwards, as if "up" was the only holy direction.

Though we admit that it may be good that, in our bodily observation, we should lift up our eyes and our hands if the spirit stirs us. But works of our spirit should neither be directed upwards nor downwards, not to one side or to the other, not forward or backward, for these are simply directions. These specified directions are merely fleshly things to do, done too often to become distracting for us. This work is spiritual only and not actual physical work, which is a bodily function meant for the flesh to manage.

THE FIFTY-EIGHTH CHAPTER

Standing in Heaven

This is what those with one foot still in this world say when they speak of either Saint Martin or Saint Steven. They speak with their worldly eyes as if they were present, acting as if these things shown to them were both miracles and certifiably spiritual things. They seem to fully understand that, in reality, Saint Martin's mantle was never worn by Christ, for he had no need to wear it to keep himself from the cold, for warmth came by that miracle. In this same way for us who are saved that, like Saint Martin, we can be united to the body of Christ spiritually. Thus, whoever clothes a poor man or does any other good deed for the sake of God's love, either in the flesh or in the spirit, serving any who have a need, surely they do it unto Christ spiritually. These shall be rewarded as substantially as if they who have done it to Christ's own body as He, Himself, says this in the Gospel. And yet He thought this was not enough, for He affirmed it again later in a miracle, and it was for this reason that He showed Himself unto Saint Martin by revelation.

Understand this: all revelations bear some physical likeness to this life, as is known by all. These revelations have spiritual meanings. Those to whom a vision was shown or those who have somehow seen such a thing have done so spiritually. This is true only if they have understood the spiritual meanings of the revelations, otherwise they would never have been shown in a physical form. Therefore, let us carefully pick through the rough bark of this issue and eat of the sweet kernel.

Certainly we will not examine this subject as the heretics we spoke of have done, those have been seen as being foolish when they follow the sort of custom that, whenever they have drunk from an attractive cup, they cast it against the wall and break it.

Rather, in our desire to do what is right in the world, this is the sort of thing we never do. We will not feed ourselves of the fruit if we despise the tree; nor should we drink and then break that cup from which we have just drunk. In this example, we shall call the tree and the cup visible miracles, as are all the revelations that are bodily observable. This is in accordance, and not a hindrance, to the work of the spirit. We must claim the spiritual meaning of the fruit and the drink to be regarded as visible miracles, as real as are these seemingly fleshly observances such as the lifting of our eyes and raising our hands unto heaven. If the stirring of our spirit does these things, then they are well done. Otherwise they are hypocrisy and they are false. But if they are true and contain the spiritual fruit, why should they be despised? For some will publically kiss the cup, but it is for the wine inside that they truly lust.

This means that our Lord, when He physically ascended into heaven, rose into the clouds even as His mother and His disciples watched with their eyes. Does this mean in our spiritual work that it is right we should forever stare upwards with our eyes, looking for Him to see if we can see Him sitting in heaven or even standing as Saint Steven saw Him? No, never, because Jesus did not show Himself to Saint Steven in the flesh in heaven so as to give us an example of how we should behave in our spiritual work. This is not our work on earth, to be always seen to be looking up into heaven on the chance that we might see Him, to see whether He is standing or sitting or lying. How His body is in heaven—whether standing, sitting, or lying—no one knows, nor should we know. We need to know only that He was raised body and soul, without separation. The body and the soul, that which Jesus has accomplished, unites us with the Godhead, now and forever, without separation. So, whether He is sitting or standing or lying, we do not need to know except to know that He is there as He said He would be, in bodily form, as is most proper for Him to be. For if He was seen to be lying or standing or sitting, as witnessed by revelation by anyone in this world, it will be shown for some spiritual purpose. But it is not shown for any purpose relating to His physical presence in heaven. We must not get physical and spiritual issues confused.

We are to stand and remain in a state of readiness to help another, but not to be staring upward. Therefore, as it was said of one friend to another as they are going to battle: "Bear yourself well in the battle, my friend, and fight hard; do not give up on the battle lightly; for I will stand with you." By this, the speaker meant he would stand with his friend, whether the battle was to be waged on horse or on foot. Perhaps it is going forth but it is not standing still. What the first friend means as he speaks to the other is that he will stand by him, he will be there always ready to help his friend.

It was for that reason only that our Lord Jesus showed Himself in heaven to Saint Steven at the time when Saint Steven was suffering his martyrdom. But in this He did not give us an example that we should be walking around looking up to heaven. As He said to Saint Steven, as in the presence of all those who have ever suffered persecution for the sake of His love, "Look, My child! As surely as I open this bodily firmament which is called heaven, and let you see Me bodily standing for you, have faith that I will, as surely, stand beside you spiritually by the might of My Godhead. I am ready to help you. Therefore, stand firmly in the faith and suffer boldly the blows of the hard stones, for I will crown you in the bliss of heaven for your reward, and not only you, but all those who suffer persecution for My sake in any manner."

By these examples, I trust you can see that these bodily showings of the Lord were done for the sake of spiritual interpretation and not as a command that we are to remain constantly looking heavenward for His return.

THE FIFTY-NINTH CHAPTER

On this Earth

If you ask anything regarding the ascension of our Lord Jesus as to whether it was done spiritually or physically, it was done in the flesh. Be aware here, what you ask about has a fleshly meaning and a spiritual meaning. He ascended as both true God and true Man; to this I offer a thought for you: He who was dead is now clothed in immortality, as we will be on that Day of Judgment. On that Day, we will be wonderfully re-made in both body and soul. Then we will quickly become whatever we desire to be in the flesh, as we can now become in our spiritual thoughts. This will be true no matter where our thoughts take us, whether up or down, to one side or to the other, behind or before. All these things shall be, we trust, as the scholars say they will be. But for now you will not be able to go to heaven in the flesh, but only in the spirit. It will be as spiritually wonderful as it can be, but not so regarding matters of the flesh which cannot travel upwards or downwards, neither on one side nor on the other, behind or before.

So it is wise to consider those who have set themselves apart to be spiritual laborers, especially those who would follow the work of the Contemplatives, as is the purpose of this book. Those who read and seek ideas such as being "lifted up" or "going in" will be disappointed, for the real purpose of this book should only be for the awakening of a stirring in your heart. However, it is good to gain a full understanding the meaning of this "stirring," to learn that it neither stretches the body nor the flesh, nor is it is a stirring as to take you from one place or another. Though it may occasionally seem that this state can be seen as a state of rest we are achieving, nevertheless, those who read and understand will not think that they will find any rest in one place without leaving that place where they now reside. For the perfection of this work is pure and spiritual within itself as it must be fully and truly understood. It can be seen from afar that this is a stirring of your heart and not a calling to any physical place in particular.

This should also, with good reason, be considered a call to a sudden changing which is more than any physical change could move you. For of time, place, and body, these three states need to be forgotten in regard to all our spiritual workings. Therefore, beware that in this work you take no exception to the bodily ascension of Christ whereby it might cause you to strain your imagination during your time of prayer. Do not allow it to cause you to try to rise bodily as if you would climb over the moon. It is not wise to try to be spiritual in such a manner. But if you could ascend into heaven in the flesh, as Christ did, then you might take example at it; but that is something no one can do but God, as Jesus Himself witnessed. The Gospel says: "There is no one who may ascend to heaven, but only the One who descended from heaven, and became human for the love of all" [John 3:13]. That is Jesus Christ, only and rightly so. But if it were possible, as it never can be, yet it would be for an abundance of spiritual purposes and not any physical purpose. Such a thing would only be possible by the might of the Spirit, far from any of our bodily stressing or straining of our fleshly imagination, either up, or in, or to one side, or to the other. Therefore, let it be seen as a falsehood, for such a thing cannot be done.

THE SIXTIETH CHAPTER

Direction of Heaven

By now, perhaps, you see how these things should be. For you may think that you have much evidence that heaven is upwards, for we know that Christ did ascend upwards in the flesh, and from there sent the Holy Spirit as He promised, coming bodily down from above, unseen by any of His disciples. This is a simplification of our Christian belief. However, do not think, seeing you know these things are true, that perhaps you should direct your mind upward during the times of your prayer? It is neither so, nor is it necessary.

Rather, say this: Since it is true that Christ ascended bodily, and thereafter He sent the Holy Spirit in bodily form, then it seems quite proper that the Holy Spirit descended from an upwards direction and from above us rather than either from a downwards direction as from beneath, behind, before, or even from one side or the other. Yet though He may have ascended, not having gone downwards rather than upwards, I dare to speak of this because the way is really so near. Spiritually, heaven is as truly downward as it is up, and upward as well as down, behind as well as before, before as well as behind, and on one side as well as on the other. In this it is so that, whoever has a true desire to be in heaven, at that same time of having that desire, such a one is in the spiritual heaven already. For the high road and the way to heaven are both paths of desire and are not to be accomplished by the simple walking pace of feet. Of this Saint Paul says, regarding himself and many others: "Therefore all our bodies have been presented here in earth, nevertheless yet our living is in heaven" [Philippians 3:20]. By this he spoke of their love and their desires, which are spiritually the same as their lives. For truly, there is a soul that loves the body and it lives inside that flesh, and thus gives it life. Therefore, if we will go to heaven spiritually, it does not need to train our spirit regarding direction, either up or down, the one side or the other. Our spirit needs to be content where it is for this time and this place.

THE SIXTY-FIRST CHAPTER

Spiritually Upright

Do not be discouraged. It is good to lift your eyes and your hands bodily toward the heavens where the elements of creation were fashioned. All that really matters is that we have been stirred by the work of our spirit; nothing else really matters. For all bodily things are eventually subjected to spiritual things; all will be revealed then, but not afterwards.

An example of this may be seen in the ascension of our Lord. When the time had come that He was physically destined to go to His Father in His fleshly form, He returned to His Father even though He was never, not ever, absent from the Godhead. He had come with power by the virtue of the Spirit of God. When He came in the flesh, it was still in union with the divine Person. The visibility of this ascension was rightly seen and was, most assuredly, to the upward.

This subjection of the body to the spirit, that is having the spirit lead the body, is the purpose of this book as it was conceived as a proof of our intentional spiritual nature. This book is aimed at those who labor to be Contemplatives. For when the soul supposes itself to be capable and effective for any work, it must act quickly—even if it does not know the scope of the labor—because the body, before the labor was begun, would rather rebel. The body would try to take itself downwards, on one path or another, seeking any easier way for the sinful sake of its own flesh. By virtue of the spirit, it must be set upright. The body must be made to follow after the manner and likeness of a body under control as the spirit inspires it. This is as it should be.

It is for this reason that we, who may be the most beautiful things that God ever created, are not made to serve the earth as are all the other beasts, but are to stand upright, raised towards heaven. This is why the body/spirit should be displayed equally, both bodily in the work of the world and spiritually in the work of the soul. That which stands upright spiritually is not spiritually crooked. Take care of these things of which we speak, for they are to be read spiritually and not bodily. For how should a soul, which by nature has of itself no manner of conflict with the flesh, strain to stand upright in the flesh? We, who stand, stand spiritually.

So beware when those things you recognize as not being bodily are truly meant to be spiritual, even though they are spoken in real words. Use these words cautiously: UP or DOWN, IN or OUT, BEHIND or BEFORE, ON ONE SIDE or ON THE OTHER. These are not spiritual words in themselves; nevertheless, they are often spoken as such since speech is a bodily work performed by the tongue. The tongue is an instrument of the body. Words, by their nature, must always be considered as bodily words. Do not allow words to be taken as evil, though they are something conceived bodily. Those of you with understanding should understand these things spiritually.

THE SIXTY-SECOND CHAPTER

God is Above You

Because you now know the difference between knowing which words have been conceived spiritually and which words have been spoken bodily, it is important for you know the spiritual meaning of the words which fall into the realm of spiritual labors. You need to know this, clearly and without error, when your spiritual work is beneath you or when it is beyond you, as opposed to when you need to understand it is within you and when it is beyond you. Then it is above you and under God.

All the things of the flesh are outside of your soul and are, thus, by nature, beneath it. Even the sun and the moon and the stars, though they seem to be over your head, nevertheless, are still beneath your soul.

All angels and all souls, although they are all conformed to God's will and have been adorned with grace and virtues, and while they have been above you in cleanliness, nevertheless, they are, by nature, your equals.

Within your nature is found the strength of your soul that consists of these three main principles: Mind, Reason, and Will; and secondarily: Imagination and Sensuality.

In nature, there is nothing above you except God.

Whenever you find anything written concerning yourself as regarding any aspect of your spiritual nature and pursuit, then it is to be understood that it is talking about your soul and not about your flesh. For it is only after you overcome these spiritual things that your soul can find the strength to work. It is by the strength of your soul's commitment that the value and the condition of your work will be judged, according to whether these things are beneath you, within you, or above you.

SECTION VIII: Mentally Arriving

THE SIXTY-THIRD CHAPTER

Mind and Body

Your mind is a strength and a power within itself. Properly speaking, your mind does not actually labor. But the mind does possess reason and will; they are its two working strengths, as are its imagination and sensuality. By these four strengths and their workings, the mind is able to contain and comprehend itself. But it cannot be said that the mind actually does work, unless you think that comprehension is work.

Some strengths of the soul can be classified as being principal and others as being secondary. The soul cannot be divided, it is not possible, but many of the aspects within its labors are divisible. Some are principal things and some are spiritual things, while other aspects are secondary. The secondary aspects consist of all things of the flesh. The two principal working strengths are Reason and Will; and these two work purely in themselves in all spiritual things without the help of the two secondary strengths. The secondary strengths, Imagination and Sensuality, work both in the flesh, whether they are actually present or not, and they work with the intellect. By them, without the help of Reason or

Will, the soul would never come to know morals or the conditions of the world in the flesh, nor the purpose of their existence.

It is for this thinking that Reason and Will are called the principle strengths, for they work in pure spirit without any manner of the flesh. Imagination and Sensuality are secondary, along with the body. They are our fleshly instruments.

These are our five wits. The mind is called a principal power for it contains that which is spiritual, but it also controls the other strengths, and therefore it contains all these things in which they labor. There is truth in this.

THE SIXTY-FOURTH CHAPTER

Reason

Reason is the strength by which we are able to divide that which is evil from that which is good. The evil comes from the worse, the good from the better; the worse comes from the worst, and the better from the best. Before sin entered the world, Reason, by its nature, would have done all this. But now Reason has become so blinded by Original Sin that it can no longer labor at this work unless it is illuminated by grace. As regarding both self-reasoning and the things in which it labors, these traits are now comprehended and contained in the mind.

Will is a strength through which we choose what is good, but only after its state is determined by Reason. Through it, we love God, we desire God, and we finally rest ourselves with the full pleasure and consent of God. Before sin entered the world, it was Strength and not Will that guided our choices in loving and in all of our works, for then these things were decided by our nature while we were free to savor each thing as it was meant to be. It is not so now, for now it may only be given through the discerning power of anointed grace. Too often, because of the infection of the Original Sin, our Will now can savor a thing, thinking it is good when, in truth, such a thing is fully evil, even though it bears the likeness of a good thing. Now both the Will and the thing that it desires are to be found only in a mind that tries to contain and comprehend it.

THE SIXTY-FIFTH CHAPTER

Imagination

Imagination is that power through which we portray all images of things, both those which are absent and those which are present. Imagination and those things that work in it are contained in the mind. Before sin entered the world, Imagination was obedient to Reason; in fact, it was then a servant to Reason. Before we sinned, it never offered any non-ordained images to any creature of the flesh or any images of fantasy to any spiritual creature. Now that is no longer true.

Now Imagination is no longer restrained by Reason or by the light of Grace; it does not cease to be active. It is the nature of sin to be active. The Imagination rests neither while you are asleep nor when you are awake. It is free to portray many non-ordained images of the flesh and as many other fantasies as it can conceive. These images have nothing to do with anything except the conceits of the flesh. This is in regard to spiritual things as well as with the spirit regarding bodily things. These images are always corrupted and false. They join together in the errors of sin.

This disobedience of the Imagination may clearly be

understood in those who have been newly turned away from the world and come, purposefully and intentionally, to a life of devotion and prayer. Before they turned away from the world, it may have seemed that their Imagination had been, for the greater part, refrained by Reason in the light of Grace. It comes with force during their continual meditation of spiritual things. When Contemplatives come to seriously consider their own wretchedness, the Passion, and the kindness of our Lord God, and many such other things that led them away from the things of the world, they begin to understand themselves better. This is when Imagination shows its real self. In time, some of them became unable to move away from the temptations of their diverse thoughts, fantasies, and images that had been printed in their minds. Curious images of the Imagination that they did not understand they carried with them. All these images are a form of disobedience; they are the result of the pain of the Original Sin.

THE SIXTY-SIXTH CHAPTER

Sensuality

Sensuality is a power within our soul that reaches out and regenerates itself through the senses of our body. By it we have knowledge of the flesh and feelings toward all other creatures of the flesh. These thoughts may be pleasant or not.

This Sensuality has two parts: one that addresses the needs of our bodies and the other that serves the lusts of the body's senses. This same power is the one that complains when the body lacks anything it feels it needs, and then, in meeting that need, stirs us to desire more than what we truly need. This is true whether it is in the feeding of our flesh or in the sating of our lusts. This Sensuality complains at the lack of creature comforts and lusts in delight at their presence. Likewise, it complains at the presence of things it dislikes while it lusts after the pleasure of their absence. Both this power and the things that are at work there are also contained in the same mind.

Before humanity sinned there was Sensuality, but it was obedient to the Will. It was a servant to the Will and it never offered any non-ordained images or complaints to any creature of the flesh. Then it never provided any spiritual feigning regarding either what it liked or disliked of any spiritual aspect of the body's senses. But now it is not so: for Sensuality is no longer ruled by the grace of the will. It will not suffer in meekness at any of the pain caused by the Original Sin. This was the same that could be felt in the absence of desires and in the presence of profitable discernment; it is no longer so. Sensuality has become a strain upon us for its lusting after something desired or from any lustful pleasure it seeks in the absence of profitable discernment. Now it can make all else seem wretchedly and wantonly desirable, not unlike the way a swine feels in the mire. It is that for which the wealthy of this world lusts more and more, like the foul flesh they have in common with the swine. Sensuality would have our living become more animal-like and fleshly than is good for either us or our spirit.

THE SIXTY-SEVENTH CHAPTER

Arriving

Now consider this, my spiritual friend! Look at the depth of wretchedness to which we have fallen. Think of what a wonder it is that we have grown to be so blinded and easily dissuaded from our understanding of spiritual words and spiritual workings. Then consider those many who do not yet know the power of their soul or the nature of its workings.

You know, whenever the mind is occupied with anything regarding the flesh, no matter to what good end is intended; you will find yourself bound in some soulless fashion to that labor. However, may it also be so that when you feel your mind occupied with the richly subtle conditions regarding the power of your soul or the workings of spiritual things, that you find this is good. When you look within yourself and upon that which you are now able to focus and then react, regardless of whether they seem to be vices or virtues, what do you see? Or what do the eyes of another who is your spiritual equal in nature see? Can you be certain it is a right thing, that this is good? Then, in the end, you begin to realize that you are further along the way of perfection than you thought. That is when you discover whether you have been straight in yourself and been true to God. If you ever feel your mind is unable to become occupied with things that are either fleshly or spiritual, but you only think of the very substance of God, this may be the proof of the rightful workings of this book. Then you may truly be in that Cloud of Unknowing, above yourself and the world while being under your God.

It is only when you are above yourself that you can know you have attained that place by grace that you could not have ever arrived by your own nature.

This is to say that, on your own, you could never hope to be united to God, either in spirit and in love, never in accordance to your own will. Although you are truly beneath your God, whatever may be said about this time with God, you are no longer two but have become one in spirit. This is true in so far as you or another may feel in such a union of the perfection of this work. This, too, is truthful, as testified by the witness of Scripture and those truly called by God. Yet no matter how far you are above the world you may seem to be, nevertheless, you are beneath God. Do not forget that God is God, the God of nature without beginning. You are something of the nothing of substance, the lump spoken of earlier. And so, after you realize you are in God's might and love, you can still be a nothing if you willfully and with sinful pride make yourself available to sin. It is only by God's mercy, and without your doing, that you have been made one with God in grace, united with God in spirit, both here and in bliss of heaven which will be without any end. So that, though you are one with God in grace, yet you are still far beneath God in nature.

Consider these things, my spiritual friend! Here you can see some of the problems for those who do not know the power of their own soul or the nature of their workings. These are those who may be completely and easily deceived into misunderstanding these very words that have been written to provide spiritual insight. Here, you may see something of the cause as to why anyone would dare to urge you not to reveal your desire unto God, but, instead, bid you to behave like a child and both hide and conceal this passion for God. This step should be done carefully with fear that you might misconceive that which is the flesh, failing to believe in that which is meant to be spiritual.

THE SIXTY-EIGHTH CHAPTER

Being Nothing

In this same manner of thought, be very careful. If another invites you to gather your powers and your thoughts entirely within yourself and thereby worship God, no matter how sincerely it sounds, even though all that one says seems right and truthful and no one you ever heard sounded truer or more sincere—yet you must learn to fear any deceit or worldly meaning in those offered words. Do not listen to such a one. This is why we say to you: you should not look to yourself or those things within yourself for solution, nor to the opinions of another. Briefly put, do not go outside of yourself, nor be above, nor behind, nor be on one side or the other seeking for answers.

You should probably ask. "Then where shall I be? Nowhere, according to what you are telling me!"

You are right to realize this. If you say this, then you truly see well, for that is exactly where you want to be. For that which is "nowhere in the flesh" is "everywhere in the spirit."

Look diligently after your spiritual work and see that it is not in the least bit worldly, for wherever that work is, that is where you should willfully labor in your mind. As sure as to where you are in spirit, there you are as certainly to be in your body. That is an unavoidable place where you find yourself bodily situated. Only in being "nowhere" will all your worldly thoughts find nothing on which to feed, for they will think that you are doing nothing. This is good! So to this nothingness go, and do it for the sake of God's love. Let there be nothing but diligent labor in that nothingness which you do, except, perhaps, for an ever-awaking desire to know God in a way that no one else can ever know. This is the truth: it is better to be nowhere in the flesh, wrestling with that blind nothing, than to be a great and noble person that you might have once desired to be. That was when you understood things only in the flesh, merrily playing the role of a lord as only a lord may play.

Let this "nowhere" be your "everywhere" and your all; let all the rest be as nothing. You can never reach this place unless your wits have no knowledge in this nothing; and that is why we love it so much. It is a very worthy thing of itself that they, who are of the world, can never comprehend. "Nothing" is better felt than seen; for it is completely incomprehensible and dark to those who have barely glanced at such things.

Nevertheless, I think it is wise to say that a soul is more blinded in its sense of feelings than it is by the abundance of spiritual light, and this is true as well for any darkness or desiring of bodily light. So, who is one who dares call it a "nothing?" Surely it is our outer self and not our inner self. Our inner self sees it all for being all, and in that understands all things, both those things of the flesh and those of the spiritual, without giving any special consideration to anything of itself.

THE SIXTY-NINTH CHAPTER

Nothingness

Our affections can be wonderfully varied regarding our spiritual feelings of this nothingness, especially when it can be nowhere found. The first time that a soul looks upon that nothingness, it seems to find all the special acts of sin it ever committed. It finds all sins that are of the flesh and spirit, secret and obscure sins are depicted there. However, when we try to look at it, those sins will always appear before our eyes until the time comes when, by much hard work and many deep sighs with much bitter weeping, they are almost rubbed away.

Sometime in our trials we may think that to look at those sins is to look into hell; for we despair, wondering if we can ever hope to reach any state of perfection in spiritual rest and escape from the pain we rightfully deserve. Many have come this far on this inward journey, but for the degree of pain that they feel and for the lack of comfort, they have returned to the ways of the flesh. Unable to bear the pain, they seek refuge in those other bodily comforts. They were those who lacked the spiritual depth that they had blindly assumed they had but had not yet received, and so they would not endure the pain.

Those who persevere eventually feel some sense of comfort and find some hope of that perfection. This happens when they begin to feel and see that many of their previously committed sins have been, in the great part, erased through the help of grace. Nevertheless, they continue to feel pain of those sins, but they come to believe that those pains will eventually end. In time it does lessen. Therefore, they realize that it is not hell but merely purgatory in which they temporarily reside. Sometimes they may find no special sin written there, yet know the weight of sin like a lump. They may never know what it is that holds them back, although generally it is nothing other than themselves. Often it may be seen to be only the remaining stump of the pain of the Original Sin. At other times they may think it is paradise or heaven where they dwell, for it is filled with diversely wonderful sweet things and comforts, for such are the joys and blessed virtues that they find there. Sometimes they think this nothing is God, for it is peace and rest they found there.

Consider what they must think God's will is; for even there, everywhere they look they will find only the great Cloud of Unknowing remains between themselves and their God.

THE SEVENTIETH CHAPTER

Discernment

It may seem strange, but you must work hard to achieve this state of nothingness and this state of being nowhere. Leaving your outward, bodily thinking is something that makes this work impossible to be understood by others.

By your eyes only, you cannot really conceive what this nothingness really is except, perhaps, its length and breadth, its smallness and greatness, its farness and nearness, and the colors of these things. By your own ears you will hear nothing but noise and the sum total of noise. By your nose you will smell nothing but stench or savor, and by your taste you will not know whether it possesses sourness or sweetness, saltiness or freshness, bitterness or delightfulness. And then, by your feelings, you will feel nothing except heat or cold, hardness or tenderness, and softness or sharpness.

For truly, neither God nor the things of the spirit possess any of these listed qualities or quantities. Therefore, leave behind your limited, outward thinking and do not labor for these things, for God is not with them.

All who see themselves as spiritual laborers also imagine that they can hear, smell, see, taste, or feel spiritual things, either within or outside themselves. They are deceived and will work wrongly against the course of nature. They have naturally ordained themselves to be creatures of knowledge to all outward things of the body, but in no way will they ever come to the knowledge of spiritual things, and certainly not by their works.

However, it is by their failings we may know that those things we read or hear spoken regarding certain spiritual things can often help us to understand what we outwardly sense. These senses, however, cannot tell us of the quality of what those things might really be. By this we may be able to be clearly assured which things are spiritual things and which are things of the flesh.

In the same fashion, this assurance happens to our senses spiritually when we struggle, trying to know God. Can we ever have so much spiritual understanding in the knowledge regarding all spiritual things and yet never, by the work of our own understanding, come to that knowledge? These are the very things that are unknowable by any except God. For in failing to understand this, the search will fail; how could it do anything but fail when its failure is by the hand of God. It was for this reason that Saint Dennis said: "The only true knowing of God is this: true knowing is found only in the unknowing."

And truly, whoever will look at the books of Saint Dennis will find that his words clearly affirm all that has been said in this book, from the beginning of this treatise to the end. Thus, there is no reason to cite him: nor are there any other writers to consider at this time. At one time others thought it meekness to say nothing of those thoughts that were in their own heads unless they affirmed it exactly by Holy Scripture or another writer's words. In time that custom has turned writing into an empty courtesy and then into a brazen showing of their own cunning without adding any insight into the spiritual quest. To you this does not need to be, and it will not do it. Those who have ears, let them hear; and whoever is stirred in the quest for knowledge, let them discern what they should know and what they should not know.

SECTION IX: Example of the Three

THE SEVENTY-FIRST CHAPTER

Aaron's State

Some think this matter of discernment is difficult, and so they are fearful of it. They say that it cannot happen without a long, hard struggle. They say it is a thing rarely conceived and then only after a long time of spiritual work will it result in ecstasy. To these doubters, the answer must be given as gently as possible, tell them that it is all according to the ordinance and disposition of God, as God sees fit. These things are done according to the abilities of the soul of the seeker in regard to how this Contemplative grace and the spiritual growth work. That is how these gifts are given.

Yet there are some who, after long and tiring spiritual exercises, have been unable to come to this point. Such an experience occurs fairly seldom and, even then, only at a special calling of our Lord. Some will never feel the perfection on this issue, a wonderful feeling that we call ecstasy. But there are others who have been subtly blessed in grace and in spirit; they are still intimate with God in this grace of Contemplation. They seem to have been able to move from whatever state they were into whatever state they wish for. This is a blessed state that was once a common state of one's soul. They can be in a state of ecstasy whether sitting, going, standing, or kneeling. Yet even in this time when they are in that state, they have full deliberation over all their senses in both body and spirit. They use their senses when they will. However, it is never without some hindrance, and sometimes with great hindrance. We have an example of this first in Moses and another example of this in Aaron, his brother, the priest of the temple.

This is why the grace of Contemplation can be observed in the example of the Ark of the Testament of the Old Law. Those who worked within this grace can be seen as those who best modeled the role of the Contemplative, as the story witnesses to us. This is how grace and work are likened to that Ark, for it is rightly stated that in the Ark were the jewels and the relics of the temple. This is not unlike how a small amount of love has been known to contain all the virtues of one's soul. The same is true in the spiritual temple of God.

Moses, before he could see this Ark and learn how it should be made, climbed to the top of the mountain, passing through long and great hardships while he dwelled in and worked in that cloud for six days. He remained there until the seventh day, at which time our Lord guaranteed his safety in order to show him how to go about the making of the Ark. Throughout those hardships, Moses further endured this until his later return. Those who have done likewise have come to understood that no one can arrive at the perfection of this spiritual work without long travail. Those who have gone through these trials claim this is true. But we also recognize that this is impossible unless God chooses to show it.

Moses did not come to this ecstasy often or easily; it was only after great and long trials. Aaron had in his power, because of his office, the opportunity to enter into the temple through the veils as often as he wished to enter. By this, Aaron's state has been understood by all those who we should wish to emulate. Such Contemplatives have always spoken of Aaron thusly. These are the same ones who, by their spiritual intelligence and by the help of the grace of God, can move properly into that state of perfection in this work as often as they liked.

THE SEVENTY-SECOND CHAPTER

Contemplative States

Consider these things spoken of. These are examples you want to consider, for one does not easily come to the Contemplative state but achieves it only after seeing and feeling the perfection of this work through great travail. Even then it is rare. Those who do achieve this state often find themselves vulnerable, easily deceived if they dared to speak about it, or worse, if such were willing to think about being in such a state may then dare to judge others as they have judged themselves. Again, such people as this are only able to come to this condition rarely, and then it is achieved with great effort. In the same way, they may inadvertently be self-deceived. Those who are able to reach this state whenever they wish may be tempted to judge others by their own standards; they might assume that anyone is able to achieve that state whenever they desire it. Instead, let this be an example of a bad example, for surely they must not think they can judge others by their own standards. This is true. Perhaps, as it is pleasing to God, some are never able to find this state of ecstasy in the first place while others, and they are rare persons, find it easily. Rarely does it come easily to those who seek it. It all comes with great effort. Again, some find that they are like Aaron and have access to that inner sanctum whenever they wish, and as often as they like. We have another example of this in Moses, to whom, at first, it seldom came and then not without those great trials on the Mountain, for he rightfully feared he might not live to see the manner of the Ark. Yet afterward he was able to see it as often as he liked, even in the valley.

THE SEVENTY-THIRD CHAPTER

Bezaleel's Role

There are three men who best modeled these conditions for us through this story of the Ark of the Covenant as found in the Old Testament: Moses, Bezaleel, and Aaron. Moses learned on the mountain how our Lord said it should be built. Bezaleel, the craftsman [Exodus 36 & 37], wrought the labor and made it in the valley after the example that was shown to Moses on the mountain. Finally, Aaron was entrusted with it. It was in his keeping in the temple, to feel it and see it as often as he liked.

In the image of these three, you can learn of three manners of this grace for Contemplatives. Sometimes we profit only by grace, and then we have been likened unto Moses, that for all the climbing and the travail that he had on the Mountain, it was only on the Mountain he might see it. This happens seldom and yet it was that sight given only by the showing of our Lord when Moses was able to bring it down from the Mountain. This was the reward of Moses' travail.

Likewise, sometimes we can profit in this grace by our own spiritual efforts, helped with grace, and then we are likened to Bezaleel. It was he who would not normally ever have seen the

Ark except that he was the one called on to build it by his own toil and labor, as he was helped with the example that was shown to Moses in the Mountain.

Sometimes we profit in this grace by the teaching of others, as we see when we have been likened to Aaron. Aaron had the task of the keeping and dressing in costume as was fit to see and feel the Ark whenever he liked. This was the same Ark that Bezaleel had labored upon and was made ready by his hands, as Moses had instructed him.

Oh, spiritual friend, look at this work and consider what it means, though occasionally such illustrations of people doing God's bidding have been thought to be both childish by those without understanding. Yet this is the truth: we are each wretched, unworthy to teach anyone about the office of Bezaleel, either regarding the making or the declaring of the labors regarding the manner of this spiritual Ark. But far better and more worthy than that, you may work as if you were Aaron, that is to say, continually working therein for yourself. If you can, then do so for the love of God Almighty. Afterwards you will find you have been called of God to work in this labor. In this, it is for God's love that fulfills your part, that very thing that is lacking in so many.

THE SEVENTY-FOURTH CHAPTER

Your Book, Only

If you decide that this manner of laboring is not in accordance with your disposition of either your body or soul, then it is wise that you leave it now, lay down this book, and take up another line of work. But do this cautiously and only after receiving good spiritual counsel that you may be found to be without any blame. The writer and the transcriber of this book would also urge you to forgive them; for in this writing they have truly hoped to share with you some of the writer's simple knowledge. This has been our only intent. Therefore, we urge you to read this book over a second and then a third time, the more the better. Consider what you read. The more you think about these things, perhaps at some place or at some time, any thought which was too hard for you on the first or second reading, you might see it later in a new and full light.

It seems impossible to our understanding that any soul who would be inclined to take on this manner of work would ever read this book, speak of it, hear it read, or hear of it being spoken of.

That same soul may feel, even for a short time, any sense of agreement with this work. However, if you think this work does you any good, thank God heartily and then, for God's love, pray for us.

Please, do! In return, the transcriber will pray for you that in God's love you will allow no one else to see this book, unless you find other like-minded searchers for God. If it happens that there is such a person who you think would like the book, even after what you have understood that what you found written in the book defines what sort of people should labor in this work, let the book be read. If you let any such people see it, then I pray that you also urge them to take their time as they look this book over. For, perhaps, they may find some matter within, whether in the beginning or in the middle, which has a conclusion left hanging and is not fully declared where it stands in the book. Warn them that if it is not clearly finished in you; let them know when they read it that soon it may be resolved. The conclusion of these thoughts might be found in the end of the book. If the reader only reads part of the book, then such a reader is lost. For if this reader sees only one part and not another, perhaps that reader will be quickly led into error. Therefore, we pray, you must do as you see right.

If you think that there are any thoughts or areas within this book that you would like to have further explained to you, let us know what it is and what your concern is so that, in our simple way, we might try to amend this shortcoming you find.

As to those worldly word janglers, flatterers and blamers, whisperers, critics, and talebearers, and all like manner of pinching souls, I hope they never get to see this book. It has never been anyone's intent to write such a thing for them. Therefore, we would have it that none of them hear of it, not them or any of those curiously literate or simply illiterate people. Although they may be good people in the pursuit of Active Living, this book is not meant for them. It is meant for Contemplatives only.

THE SEVENTY-FIFTH CHAPTER

A Final Word

To all those who read or hear of the matters of this book or to those to whom these matters have been read or spoken: if you, in the reading or hearing of these things, think it is a good and wonderful thing to begin the work of becoming a Contemplative, be cautious. Such people must know that their reasoning alone or hunger for things of God are not enough to cause them to believe they are hearing a call of God on their lives to labor in this work of being a Contemplative. They must know that this may be only a pleasant stirring that they feel at the time of this reading; or, perhaps, this stirring comes more from their natural curiosity of their own mind more than from any calling to grace.

Test this stirring when it comes; you alone will know if this is truly the work to which you are called. First, examine yourself to see what work you have been engaged in, being certain that this will enable you to stand, with a clean conscience, before the judgment of the Holy Church. Accept whatever decree the Church's Counsel-Judges would deem most fitting in your case. If this is the entire case, it is well done. If their counsel is good, it is well received. However, if these same ones who would have you stand before the Church, if they counsel with your request to draw even closer, let them first examine themselves to see if there is anything that would hinder their judging you. If there is anything that is more pressing on their minds than your spiritual question that lies before them, let them withdraw from judging you. For if they find there is anything that they do or have done, either bodily or spiritually, they must judge themselves first. This is that which is a sufficiently good witness of their conscience; let them prove that this little love is, in a spiritual manner, the chief of all their work. If this then is how they feel—then let it be seen as a token that they, too, have been called of God to this work. Surely there is nothing better beyond this work.

I do not say that your sense of call will last forever or even that it will dwell in your minds continuously, although this may be the work to which you have been called to labor. This is never predictable. For too often the actual feelings are withdrawn from young, spiritual apprentices involved in this work for many reasons; sometime because they lacked the humility needed and only thought that it was, in the greater part, to be within their own power. If they thought they would be able to do whatever they wished and when they wished, they were wrong. Such thinking is pride. Whenever the feeling of grace is withdrawn, pride is the cause; this is not only that pride which is familiar, but also that pride that will continue to grow more intensely even after the feeling of grace has been withdrawn. Such thinking often turns the hearts of young fools into thinking that God is their enemy when, in truth, God is their best friend.

Sometimes this sense of call to be a Contemplative is withdrawn for reason of one's own recklessness. When that happens, you will soon feel a bitter pain that wracks your soul deeply. Sometimes our Lord Jesus will purposely delay His withdrawing of this grace for the sake of a plan known only to Himself. Or it is possible that the growth caused by such a delay, the one in question is one who will grow and hold God with even more esteem. Some find their renewed love sweeter than when it was newly found, and so, when they feel it again, that which had long been lost, they rejoice more deeply.

This is one of the most ready and sovereign tokens that a soul may witness, this understanding whether one has been truly called or not to labor in this work. If one feels, after any delay, a strong sense of lacking from not doing this work for a time, when it comes suddenly as it usually does, it is in the form of some joy that cannot be purchased by any means on our own part. That one so chosen will probably burn with a greater fervor of desire and a greater longing of love to labor in this work than he/she would have ever had before. This is been shown to be true so often that those who are called in this manner know the calling has more joy in the finding. This call can be renewing to the one chosen. It will reveal more joy than what anyone would have felt in their sorrow of apparently losing the call. If that is the case, surely it is a token, without error, that this call of God to labor in this work is real, no matter who such a person is who is called, or what they might have been.

For God does not look upon you through merciful eyes to see who you are or what you have been, but God sees you as you will be. As Saint Gregory witnessed, "All holy desires grow during delays; but if they wane in the delays, then they were never holy desires." If those who thought they were called find less joy and less peace in their new surroundings, with a lessened sense of purpose with any new desires, then this is proof that they were called by their natural desires. By this they know they were never possessors of an authentic holy desire. Of this holy desire Saint Augustine says, "All the life of a good Christian is nothing less than a holy desire."

So farewell, my goodly, ghostly friend. We bid you filled with God's blessing and mine! We beseech the Almighty God, who knows you, that you find counsel and spiritual comfort in God with an abundance of grace, evermore with you, and with all of God's lovers on earth. Amen.

HERE ENDS THE CLOUD OF UNKNOWING.

APPENDIX

The following paragraph was removed from the fifty-fifth chapter of the text. It contained material that the transcriber/paraphraser openly questioned regarding the spirituality of the message. For a document written in the late 1300s, it was permissible. But, as a side note, the transcriber now refrains from looking up the single nostril of anyone with a brain of fire he encounters. Consider:

An example of this may be seen in a single case rather than referring to any number of other instances. This example being that there are some disciples of necromancy, the foul practice that contains the evil science to summons dead and evil spirits. To some who have called upon the devil, a fiend has appeared in bodily form with a single nostril that is large and wide. With that single nostril he will gladly look upward so that the one for whom he came may look up that nostril and see the devil's brain in his head. That brain of the devil is nothing but the fire of hell, for a fiend like this may have no other brain. If he should entice a man to look up his nostril, there is nothing more to do, for in the looking up the nostril of the devil, the one who looks will lose his mind forever. But a careful apprentice of necromancy knows this in advance and will not look at the fiend's brain so that he does not harm himself.

A BIT OF A BIBLIOGRAPHY

Halcyon Backhouse, ed., *The Cloud of Unknowing*. (London: Hodder and Stoughton, 1985).

Dr. Phyllis Hodgson, *The Cloud of Unknowing*. (London: Oxford University Press, 1944).

William Johnston, ed., *The Cloud of Unknowing*. (New York: Image Books: Doubleday, 1973).

Ira Progoff, *The Cloud of Unknowing*. (New York: A Delta Book: Dell, 1957).

Clifton Wolters, *The Cloud of Unknowing and Other Works*. (London: Penguin, 1961).

Robert Way, *The Cloud of Unknowing and The Letter of Private Direction*. (Wheathampstead: Anthony Clarke, 1986).

Sample page from the *Study Guide for The Cloud of Unknowing* for this text.

Section II: Words

The Cloud of Unknowing   CHAPTER SIX: Stay in the Cloud (pp. 31-32)

Review: We have shared a quick introduction to the three clouds, one where God dwells, one where we dwell, and the third, the world we are trying to leave behind. The following ten chapters, "Section II: Words," give us tools and encourage us to develop skills to carry on with our quest to move closer to God.

Today's Reading: May I share some wisdom with you: Stay in the Cloud. People in our life will beat us down with their logic and common sense about why we should not seek God. They will take arrows to shoot at us from their quivers of fear. They will claim to want to protect us, but they are only trying to keep us at their level. It is hardest when those we love, family and best friends, try to talk "reason" to us. In truth, God is the reason you dare to grow. Stand firm and stay in the cloud.

Questions: Taken from the reading, complete the following sentences with a short answer.

1. The most common answer about God is to say: "_____."
2. _____ is where we want to reside.
3. Through grace, this is _____ where one may come to a full understanding.
4. Consider God, even as you realize _____.
5. Leave all the things _____ and instead chose to love God.
6. While God may be loved, _____.
7. God may be found by love and held by our hearts but _____.
8. Seek to pierce that _____ that is above you.
9. Do not _____, no matter what happens.

Discussion Questions:

10. Here is a phrase of honesty: "I don't know." When it comes to understanding God and the ways of God, we cannot declare that we understand God. We can believe with a full heart and not understand. This will forever be true in this lifetime. Sadly, in today's world, many of us are taught never to say, "I don't know," as if it implied ignorance. Regarding the things of God, it's the best we can do. It's OK to say, "I don't know." It's the right thing to say, especially if you don't know. Have you said those words or, maybe worse, didn't say them when it would have been better to speak the truth? **If you're willing, please relate any story when you should have said, "I don't know," instead of pretending that you did know.**

11. Much of our churchly knowledge of God is based on ancient traditions and old artwork. Be aware: nothing but the Spirit can reveal the magnificence of God to you. Imagine your favorite image of God. **What description of God makes you happiest?**

12. We find God in our heart, the center of our well being, not in our head. To believe without seeing is called faith. It varies, but how would you rate your faith on a scale of one-to-ten? By staying in the Cloud, your faith will grow. **Explain your heart-felt faith to someone who sincerely asks you.**

Final Word: My faith is my compass. My home is in the Cloud of Darkness, my past is in the Cloud of Forgetting, and my path now leads me to the Cloud of the Unknowing. I will stay in the Cloud and I will seek the way into the Cloud of Unknowing. My success is found in God's love for me. Amen.

SEE OTHER CREATESPACE BOOKS BY MARVIN KANANEN:

AFRICA 2013: Afoot and Lighthearted: Tanzania and Ireland. 2013. #4354721. Also available on Kindle.

WALKING WITH BASHŌ. 2015 Also available on Kindle.

BAD THEOLOGY: Short Stories Meant to Shake the Rigid and Challenge the Spineless. 2013. #4439145. Also available on Kindle.

STUDY GUIDE for *The Cloud of Unknowing*. For Marvin Kananen's 2013 translation of *THE CLOUD OF UNKNOWING*. 2019. Also available on Kindle.

ABOUT THE AUTHOR:

Marvin Kananen is a Christian, a Lutheran by denomination, born in Laurium in Michigan's Upper Peninsula, educated at Suomi College (now Finlandia University), Pacific Lutheran University, and Oakland University. He currently lives in Washington State. Now retired, Kananen has been a life-long teacher (although he has not taught every year), having taught at elementary, high school, and university levels. After his last twelve working years, he ended his teaching career (English, mostly) in 2010, concluding his working years as a missionary at the Maasae Girls Lutheran Secondary School in Tanzania. Surprisingly and wonderfully so, he is happily married, attends church regularly, and lives in Bellevue, Washington.

44,855 words.

Made in the USA
Middletown, DE
22 March 2023

27374033R00120